Crannóg 53 autumn 2020

Editorial Board

Sandra Bunting
Ger Burke
Jarlath Fahy
Tony O'Dwyer

ISSN 1649-4865
ISBN 978-1-907017-58-2

Cover image: *Étrangénique – Strangenetic*
Medium: *huile sur toile - oil on canvas*, by Béatrice Mecking
Cover image sourced by Sandra Bunting
Cover design by Wordsonthestreet
Published by Wordsonthestreet for Crannóg magazine @CrannogM
www.wordsonthestreet.com @wordsstreet

All writing copyrighted to rightful owners in accordance with The Berne Convention

Reprinted November 2020

CONTENTS

Guff
Fred Johnston 6
The Pier Head, Last Time
Maria Isakova Bennett 8
Au Revoir, Mo Chroí
Miceál Kearney 9
Distancing
David Butler 10
Rescue
Honor Duff 14
Destinations
Knute Skinner 15
Petrichor
Stephen de Búrca 16
Catching Air
Vincent Glynn-Steed 17
Without the Light Pollution We Can See the Stars
Alison Wells 18
Sounds of Mortality
Ruth Quinlan 21
Lockdown Notes April 2020
Máiríde Woods 22
Shergar's Ghost
Gerard Hanberry 23
Men of the South *Sean Keating 1921– 22*
Mary Melvin Geoghegan 24
4708 Hannaford Drive
Hanahazukashi 25
Metastasis
Bernie Crawford 30
To Answer Their Question
Anne Tannam 31
Time
Emily Cullen 32
The Grind
Caroline Graham 34
To a Friend Who is Sad and Far Away
Deborah Bacharach 38
Two Deaths
Michael Brown 39
Unearthed
Edel Burke 40
Percussion
Laura Treacy Bentley 42
Ireland's Eye
Dylan Brennan 44
The Middle of the Night, A Dark Hallway
John Higgins 45

The Seventeenth of May
   Fiona B. Smith 49
Holidays
   Iain Twiddy..54
Quarantine II
   Kate Quigley...56
Scapegoats
   Peter Branson 57
A Season of Picking Up
   Lynn Caldwell 58
Simply Meeting for Coffee
   Frank Dullaghan 60
Bully #6
   Rory Duffy..61
Garden Shed
   Cian Ferriter 62
Cursing Stone
   Billy Fenton..63
The Sin Collector
   David C. Hall..64
For the One Who Has Lived Too Little and Too Long
   Kevin Higgins 66
Skins
   Fiona Nic Dhonnacha...68
Reading the Runes
   John D. Kelly 70
No Answers
   Gerard Smyth..71
Trees Begin to Loosen
   Mercedes Lawry..72
Bright May Morning
   Patrick Kehoe...73
The Housewife's Ars Poetica
   Adina Kopinsky..74
Last Night
   Rachel Morton 76
From Montdevergues Asylum
   Úna Ní Cheallaigh..78
Wasps
   Rachel Parry...80
Intangible
   Mary Rose McCarthy 81
Within Two Kilometres
   Sighle Meehan 86
Rendezvous
   Giles Newington 88

The Garden of Earthly Delights
Fiona Pitt-Kethley 89
Someday I'll Love Susan Rich
Susan Rich 90
Visualisation
Lisa C. Taylor 92
Homing Salmon
Niamh Twomey 94
Growing Pains
Anne Walsh Donnelly 95
Frances Farmer So You Wanna Be in Pictures
Kevin Kiely 96
Loose Rock
Ellen Kelly 98
Artist's Statement
Béatrice Mecking 103

Biographical Details 104

Submissions for Crannóg 54 open November 1st until November 30th 2020
Publication date is March 27th 2021

Crannóg is published bi-annually – in spring and autumn.

*Submission Times: Month of **November** for spring issue. Month of **May** for autumn issue.*

We will <u>not read</u> submissions sent outside these times.

POETRY: Send no more than three poems. Each poem should be under 50 lines.

PROSE: Send one story. Stories should be under 2,000 words.

We do not accept postal submissions.

*When emailing your submission we require **three** things:*

1. *The text of your submission included both in body of email and as a Word attachment (this is to ensure correct layout. We may, however, change your layout to suit our publication).*
2. *A brief bio in the third person. Include this both in body and in attachment.*
3. *A postal address for contributor's copy in the event of publication.*

For full submission details, to learn more about Crannóg, to purchase copies of the current issue, or take out a subscription, log on to our website:

www.crannogmagazine.com

Guff

Fred Johnston

The young have it –
Let's face it, after sixty, draw the curtains
It's getting darker earlier
We're losing more light each waking day
Forget what the tabloid gurus say
This is not the age for climbing mountains.

The young are beautiful –
In ways we once knew well and gloried
In, primped, garrulous and glib
We haunted ourselves in every glass
Untouchable, thin and sharp as grass
We held that freedom was not being married.

The young know it all –
But we rock to the tick-tock of a cancer
Or the medical definition of a broken heart
A pain in the head that's not from booze
But something monstrous, a bloody ooze
Knowing this we fear both question and answer.

The young are wise –
We aren't; nostalgia's not wisdom, it's rot
To think we've stored up some gnostic treasure
We must spend in boring them utterly fuckless –
They do with flair and more often what luckless
Young gits like us groped after, then forgot.

The young will carry us
Up the stairs, if we're still continent enough
And take the dog for a walk when we dread the park
They talk in X-Box – we talked in Sartre –
And lied to girls that we knew all about Art
Or the Isle of Wight. Draw the curtains. Life's all guff.

The Pier Head, Last Time

Maria Isakova Bennett

We became all feathers falling,
and we became play – falling
among razor shells along the shoreline.
There is always chance, a bet,
threat, possibility. Last time was black-glass,
him walking toward a halo of streetlights,
me, back to the river, the Liver clock tolling,
passing galleries, museum, cobblestones, toward
rusted chains strung with lovers' padlocks.
Us separating, our happiness stranded
where we parted

Au Revoir, Mo Chroí

Miceál Kearney

It wasn't the loss of custom
that had every shop closed.
Staff and owner: black and bowed
towing their piece of the road.
Streets start and stop with another line
of sorry shoes until the sweet page
is returned to carbon:
living forever in the air.

Distancing

David Butler

IN PROPORTION AS THE CALL WENT ON, the knot in Emily's gut tightened. She couldn't take the chance that Betty Beglin might simply hang up, smiling bemusedly (as Emily supposed), not knowing there was a deathly serious purpose to the call. She couldn't take the chance *he* might come back, early.

But of all things, Emily hated confrontation. Interaction of any kind made her apprehensive. Sometimes, approaching a hairdresser's or a shoe shop in the days when one could still do such things, she'd actually caught herself practising in a low voice what she was going to ask for, as though she were back on her year abroad in France. A knock at the door or a ringing phone, and dread would turn a sudden somersault. Why could people not just text?

Betty Beglin could talk for Ireland. Her chatter had already dragged on so long Emily's latte was cold. Coffee had been a mistake. Her fingers, caffeine-quickened, were all a-jitter even as she'd dialled, so that it had taken two goes before she'd got the number right. But now that Betty had stopped banging on about whatever it was she'd been banging on about while Emily's innards were squirming like eels approaching a saucepan, the lengthening silence was ten times worse.

And at any moment, Frankie really might return.

She looked out over Crossthwaite Park. No sign of him. No Joxer straining at the leash. She swallowed a dry dribble of saliva. 'I meant to ask,' she tried to compose her features to approximate facetiousness, 'how's that new au pair working out?'

'Toni? She's fab! The girls are crazy for her.'

Toni. *Antônia*. That was it! 'Yeah?' Her heart fluttered skyward, a lark startled from long grass. 'She's very *young*, no?'

'The company said she was eighteen. Yeah. I'm pretty sure, eighteen. Gi-*nor*-mous family back in São Paulo, eight or nine I think she told us, so she's well used to having bundles of youngsters pulling out of her the whole time. *A cambada*, she calls them. She's a scream, a real live-wire. But honestly, she's been marvellous. I mean Shona I can understand. Shona takes to everyone. But Pauline? For the longest time they thought Pauline was,' her voice dropped to a confidential whisper, as though there might be an eavesdropper, '*On the spectrum*. Can you imagine! Pauline? She's shy, that's all. Shy! You know? I don't see why a child isn't allowed to be shy these days. But ever since Toni Oliveira arrived, she's a different kid. Right from the get-go, she took to her. Of course it helped that Shona took to her, first. She often takes her lead from Shona. You see her English isn't great, I mean Toni's, but then I suppose that's what has her over here, to improve. I mean she's forever saying things like, "I didn't went". You see? "I didn't *went*." It's kinda cute, really. And Shona thinks it's hilarious, but instead of getting annoyed about it, Toni sorta plays along. Makes a game of it. And then Pauline joins in, all giggles. I mean it's lovely to see her, giggling away and spanking poor Antônia's behind. But really, she's marvellous. I can't praise her highly enough. And *George*! George is mad about her ...'

Had she stopped for breath once in all that paean, while Emily's breath had been shallow and rapid and ineffective? *George is mad about her.* Well that about said it all. 'But she must miss her home, no? Especially now, with all this ...'

'Oh God! Bra-*zil*!?? You should just hear her on the subject of that *bobo* they have for a president over there. *Bobo*. That's what she calls him. I can't think of his name but she says he's like a Latino version of Trump. Get this! But without Trump's class! Ha! Ha!'

Emily took a breath. She took a slow, deep breath. She held it in till it hurt. Then she exhaled, entirely. OK. Calmness. 'But wouldn't she have to be studying over here, isn't that the deal? Doesn't their visa depend on them studying here, too?'

'But that's just it! The language school has been marvellous. They run these online classes. Zoom, the same thing George is using for his conference calls. Look, Emily, I better leave you go. I have about a zillion things to be doing this morning ...'

Now or never. Say it! *Say* it, for Christ's sake. 'Betty. Look. Can I ask you something?' Heartbeat. Heartbeat. 'A ... *favour*?'

'Sure. Ya! What is it?'

'She, ahm.' Say it! 'She's walking around ...,' say it, dammit! '... in these short little pants and, and a singlet. And no bra, like it was ... And with her belly on show for everyone to admire ...'

An unimpressed pause. A shift in the barometer. 'That's the Brazilians, Emily. They're like that. Every one I've met, anyway. They're young, God's sake! And the way the weather's been, well! Hasn't it been just *mar*-vellous? The Dublin Riviera, George calls it ...'

Knee-length boots? In a heatwave you don't wear knee-length boots! Not when you're eighteen. Now that she was stepping off the precipice, Emily's voice hardened. 'Then can you ask ... Antônia ... not to be hanging around Crossthwaite Park every evening? Couldn't she use, I dunno, the People's Park, or somewhere? It'd be a lot nearer to your place, for starters.'

A hostile static met Emily's request. Betty Beglin was just the type to take this for a social snub, whereas that was the last thing on Emily's mind. 'I mean it's ridiculous. It's not like any of them are social distancing. They're hanging around together like they were at Electric Picnic, or something ...'

'What's this about? What exactly has got up your nose, Emily? Toni has no more harm in her than any Irish girl her age.'

Now Emily was fired up. Annoyed. True, she was annoyed at her own lack of composure, her own lack of sleep in recent days as images and arguments tumbled like laundry through her mind throughout the small hours. But at least she was able to channel it now. Heart pounding, she took up the gauntlet. 'Well, she clearly doesn't know the first thing about social distancing. Yesterday evening, when Frankie was out walking Joxer, she stood there in her hot-pants not two feet in front of him, never mind two metres. Flashing her teeth up at him. Big, bubbly laugh out of her, I could hear it though we're at the other side of the park. I even saw her squeeze Frankie's bicep.'

A stony silence. She could all but hear Betty Beglin's smile freeze to a Botox rictus. 'Emily. Can I suggest, if you've a problem with Frankie talking to Toni, then perhaps you should take it up with Frankie, no?'

A heart murmur. A trapped bird. 'Betty,' her voice scarcely there. 'Could you not just *ask* her?' Because she couldn't say it to Frankie. She daren't. '*Please?*' Not after what happened last time she'd reproached him for his free-and-easy manner. Not now, when he was fearing for his job, and tramped round the house all day like a caged animal.

'Emily. OK. Listen to me.' Her tone had altered again. Another barometer-shift. To something like concern. 'Has he …?' Because Betty had seen. Last year. After he'd …

'Emily, if Frank has said or, or … *done* anything to you, you have to report …' But Emily wasn't listening. The hall door had swung shut, shuddering the hall and bannisters. The thud resounded like a gunshot through her chest cavity.

As Joxer's nails spilled like a hundred ball-bearings across the parquet floor, as he blundered upward toward the mezzanine, Emily plunged the phone deep into her pocket. She clamped her eyes shut, inhaled, composed the smile to meet their return; the smile that, ever since the lockdown started, seemed only to put Frankie on edge.

Rescue

Honor Duff

(i.m. Peter Bird, record-breaking lone oarsman, lost at sea 1996)

Insistent as a lover,
the sea called him
time and time again,
and he was helpless
as a Selkie trying to live
between two elements.

When at last the ocean
claimed him, spitting back
with scorn the fragile boat
to show its power and prove
this final time would not
bring the hoped-for rescue

his son Louis, aged just five
when the oarsman left,
embarked at twenty-four
questing his father's ghost,
tossing restless and alone
through giant Pacific waves.

From Monterey to Hawaii,
he rowed, obsessed but happy
on an inner rescue mission,
succeeded, and buoyed up,
announced with joy, to all:

'I brought my father safely back to land'.

Destinations

Knute Skinner

When we reached our intended destination,
it was not what we had intended,
and in time we were never quite sure
what we did intend.

We did know where we had come from.
Well, some of us knew this,
some of the time.
Was it what we wished to remember?

What we wished to remember was what
we would have remembered
if we'd come from some other somewhere
and had found some other destination.

But we did come from where we came from,
and our destination was always
the one intended for us –
for all of us, all of the time.

Petrichor

Stephen de Búrca

The sky dyes itself a lustral grey
and Spanish moss adheres to the last
impression of slash pines. I crack

a window for crisp air, but even it's
in a petrified sweat. Outside, the firebush
is crimson – only yesterday

a hummingbird came to do the rounds,
the flute-like flowers funnelling out
all but the beak, guarding the nectar

as if it were ichor. Then, the crow:
hellbent, urging the stalk to crook,
it plucked the flowers two or three

per pluck till the stalk-heads were like
gorged ears of corn. The first rain falls;
gluttonous, fat, anaemic drops. The
sparrows

swoop through the redolent air and rest
with Pitys in the pines. Earth's
sizzling roads
are held forlornly, skyward, cut from wrist

to antecubital fossa. A mosquito seeks
refuge inside. The world is fucked –
I shut the window so Pan can't be
heard.

Catching Air

Vincent Glynn-Steed

From an upstairs window I hear the procession
moan of horns, tyres jawing gravel,
the sound of car doors like a round of applause
from the gods
and then the silence
but for rustle of rose, orchid, hyacinth
and the people who tend their box of whispers
the birch trees lurking in corners, four heavenly kings
who watched us through time, settle with the mandible
of a wild boar, faces turned towards the rising sun
some bare-breasted artefact a guide in bewildering dark
to this point where a slab and stone border defines a memory
sustenance for all our ghosts
like a child catching air with a butterfly net
or dreams of the astral cartographer
– ordnance survey of stars not yet discovered.

Without the Light Pollution We Can See the Stars

Alison Wells

MORRISON WAS WITH EMILY NOW. Mornings in the garden, stepping together from the far sides of a dazzling and billowing white sheet, losing each other among the wind-lifted fabric then finding each other again. These were ordinary, wonderful things in a new life that had been decided with hardly any words needed.

In the evenings – in this garden of the rundown cottage Emily had fled to – the thing that made Morrison happiest was the stars.

He did not know the names of stars like a poet should, he could not pick them out, even five or six from the billions. Narrowing it down to the brightest ones that were planets, Jupiter, Venus or Mars, he could make a stab at it with a one in three chance.

A one in three chance, of dying from cancer, like Emily's mother, of Emily finding the right man from a trio of candidates, her husband (ex), the rebel Eddie, and the poet – him.

Without the light pollution he could see the stars. In the night, blazed awake by mind meteors he went down, quietly, to the garden. On the right nights, so serendipitously that he felt a pain in his chest, shooting stars streaked hotly through the sky.

And he stood there breathless in the moment after. Shooting stars so random and chaotic, so lovely and right, like the ideas and sensations that came at him from nowhere, from which he would then write.

The stars are senseless, he jotted down in his notebook, blind in the country dark, hoping the writing would be legible in the daytime.

He had a dreadful memory, hence the notebook and its recordings, sightings of Emily, fleeting wisps of phrases in the twilight, grasped like smoke and caught in a glass.

He could hear the trickle of the river and the great dark air was around him and the sigh let old emptiness out. Now his chest expanded again with the peace of the place and the reality of Emily lying upstairs in the cottage asleep and the girls who now called him Dad though he hadn't asked for it.

He sat, his feet amid moss and ferns, his bare toes cool in the grass.

He felt so young and endless here, out in the night, balanced at a moment that was right. He had not aimed for the stars, so he'd not fallen short. He'd worked in normal jobs, still had a mum and dad. He'd not had Emily's pain; losing her mother, extricating herself from a husband who fought with life. Though he found he could somehow understand her ex-husband, wary and blind to pleasure, to light.

The stars are senseless

He was always on the lookout for wonder, ever since he was young, always, long before he finally moved out here with Emily, Amy and Hannah. He'd always been beguiled by the romanticism of stars, their beautiful mystery, though they were so far away, or dead already. And yet the stars suggested some great white plain, beyond the dark. Some heavenly elsewhere.

Hinting, bright
At some great, blinding cloth
The opposite of night

Further back in time, there had been that day he saw Emily and her daughters on the long, unending beach of sparkling white sand. His future family.

White sands so soft and pulverised with time
And light, this aching light

Even though it took much longer until they were together, he recognised the moment on the beach as coming home, a kind of ballast, a landing. Now he sat on an immovable stone, the dark clear air all around. He saw a satellite traverse the sky.

Those tiny stars; hope stabbing through the dark

Since being with Emily he'd begun to look at people, not just fern heads and patterns in the sand. In the summer, back at his childhood estate, all the people gathered on the green chatting and children running about in swimming costumes with hoses and ice-cream. The sky was so hazy and bright, the sun was so strong and white hot. He had shielded his eyes with his hands and sunspots danced on the inside of his eyes. Those beautiful faces around him, alive and delighted – the relief and flutter of conversation was like some exotic flower bud opening out.

Twinkle, the nursery rhyme said of the stars in the book of his new stepdaughter. He was not a parent but he could feel a new kind of love shine out of him for the child. He'd hugged the mother of the little boy on the estate who'd been run over and killed. Sometimes the black cloth of the sky was all you could see, nothing else.

But out here, outside of the city and its noise and threat on a clear night you could see the white of stars shining through as if from a bright expanse of white behind, like the sands on the beach on the day he'd seen his future family.

There was now a brightness in his life that he wasn't used to. Although nothing was forever.

The stars are senseless
Hinting, bright
At some great blinding cloth
The opposite of night
White sheets flung on a summer washing line
White sands soft, pulverised with time
And light, this aching light …
Those tiny stars; hope stabbing through the dark

Morrison sat in the garden, the sky garlanded with those pinpricks of stars. He thought of how somewhere else the Earth shone for others, on this planet of random joy and tragedy. He thought of himself and Emily in daylight folding the sheets from the washing line together, walking towards each other at each fold, and then stepping away once more.

Sounds of Mortality

Ruth Quinlan

The Ontario Science Centre has a tunnel
that eliminates noise, amplifies the imperfect
clicks and wheezes of our body's machinery
till it deafens. Nobody stays too long,
chased out by the sounds of mortality.

We ache for silence, a gagging
of the frantic crowd, sliding
below the bath waterline
to stop our ears with liquid
in a return to prenatal peace.

But we keep each refuge brief –
the beat of a heart resembling
too closely the tireless rhythm
of Charon's oars, dipping as he steers
towards us, waiting beside the river.

Lockdown Notes April 2020

Máiríde Woods

I feel the loneliness of the online writer
stifling incorrect thoughts, lobbing flabby words
against a wall of self. The news is bad
yet un-put-downable: surges in cases,
unflattened death curves, comment horror. New acronyms
strut their stuff while power rides cloaked
in common good and medical necessity.

Back home the texts pile up. Concern and farce:
long-distance tales of tedious days and wicked folk
who met with friends in cordoned beauty-spots. I hate
the all together ethos, the shared tut-tuts
the way the national flag of us is wrapped
around top-down solutions. Home alone, I silence
the guilt-trip ads. How far did you go to exercise?
Yet most trade liberty for stay-safe hope
or full cocooning. In the long nights
I aim my telescope beyond the zooming darkness,
In search of some escaped and dangerous star.

Are you all right out there?

Shergar's Ghost

Gerard Hanberry

It began in the usual way,
Tom trying to have one up on us all.

He mentioned he saw Christy Ring playing for Cork
and chatted to him after in the car park.

I told him I met Bobby Charlton with the trophy
in London after they won the World Cup in '66.

Then Mick behind the bar went in the back,
returned with a framed photo of himself with Ali.

Patrick was quiet as he usually is these days,
not much life in him since he buried Muriel,

but he caught my eye in the mirror and winked,
I'll trump the lot of you, he said.

This was more like the Patrick of old.
He slipped a photograph from his wallet,

himself and Muriel in Bundoran.
Look at that, he said, look at the sky.

There's myself and herself with Shergar's ghost.
Sure enough, a cloud in the shape of a horse's head.

We had a good laugh at that. The first time
he mentioned her in the seven sad months.

Men of the South

Sean Keating 1921 – 22

Mary Melvin Geoghegan

In a world of near and far things
There's their profile –
on a new commemorative stamp.

Like figures from an ancient Greek fresco
six men with a laurel tree and
a landscape in green, white and gold.
Painted during a truce
in the Irish War of Independence
depicted as members of the North Brigade:
Jim Riordan, Denis O'Mullane, Jim Cashman,
John Jones, Roger Kiely and Dan Browne.
Having invited the men to his studio in Dublin
later, Keating would say:

'they trooped in dressed and armed
very much as they might have been
on many an ambush'.

4708 Hannaford Drive

Hanahazukashi

GRANDPA WALKS SLOWER THAN ANYONE I have ever seen. Mama and Papa told us that we have to be prepared for Grandpa to die because he is very, very sick, that the hospital let him go home so he can have a peaceful summer with family. He was skinny, but some sickness made his belly blow out big. It seems sort of hollow, and even Grandpa acts like it's something he just tacked on, the way he moves about the cucumber plants, hitting them with his tummy.

'Maybe we could get some cukes too …' He's biting his lower lip as he inspects the leaves. Even though his hair is white now, his eyebrows are full and dark brown, showing his focus.

'Grandpa, are you okay? You look serious.' His eyes soften and turn toward me, his friendly grin coming back. The blue of his eyes is wet again.

'Here, Dad, let's look at the tomaytas,' and she takes him by the elbow.

'I was just looking at the cucumbers. Wouldn't be too hard to plant a row of them. Maybe … okay, let's look at the tomatoes.'

Grandpa's backyard, years before. Rows of cucumbers and eggplants. Beds of string beans, radishes, carrots. Bushes of raspberries and strawberries. After one summer in Toledo, I asked Papa to plant strawberries in the backyard. He said they wouldn't grow in South Texas, but I pleaded and he built a bed just like one Grandpa had. But after we bought the saplings and planted them, the green baby strawberries burned right up.

Today, we end up with big boys, better boys, early girls, and big beefs, which sound more like team names than four different types of tomatoes, three more kinds than I knew there were. When we pass the cucumbers again with the cart, Mama asks, 'Dad, you still want a cucumber plant? You got a big project here already.'

Mama told me the night before, 'Don't push Grandpa, he's very weak.'
 'We don't need to plant things at all.'
 'No, no, I think it's good you asked him, but, he won't be able to do a lot. You'll have to help him do the planting.'
 'I can.'

Grandpa inspects the plants up and down and licks his bottom lip slowly.
 Mama and I look at each other and wait. Eduardo is watching Grandpa's face, and then reaches out and hugs his leg. Grandpa looks down. 'Hello, there.' He reaches to pick him up, then probably remembers he can't, and pats Eduardo's hair instead.
 'I love you, Grandpa.'
 'Love you too, Eduardo.' Grandpa looks up at my mother and seems scared all the sudden; the skin in his cheeks goes inward instead of outward, like it's trying to cling on to muscle that isn't there. He makes the face he's been making more and more often, like he is about to cry, but really it's a smile, you can tell by the way his eyes shine. 'I think we got enough,' he tells Mama.
 'Okay, Dad.'

We are supposed to plant the tomatoes when we get home, but Grandpa is tired. 'Mama, can Eddie and I go to the park?'
 'By yourselves?' She's writing at the dining room table.
 'Just to swing for a bit, before lunch?' Mama seems freer with us here, in her old home. Even though she is taking care of Grandpa, even though it is a sad task.
 'I guess so. Will you take care of Eddie?'
 'I will take care of Bala!' Eduardo shouts from the living room.
 Mama laughs. 'Okay, but lunch is in twenty minutes.'
 'What are we having?'
 She smiles and taps her fingertips together in an evil, plotting way. 'Sandwiches.'
 We giggle. Because Papa isn't around Mama doesn't have to cook at all. We eat spaghettios, mac 'n' cheese, and sandwiches. For dinner, hash browns, tater tots, or frozen pizza with frozen vegetables. It hardly takes any time.

'It's strange to play in the middle of the day,' I say to Eduardo, as we walk down Hannaford Drive toward the park.

'Mhhm!' He looks up at me, suddenly frowning. 'Will we have to shower when we get home?'

'I don't think so. It's not as hot here as McAllen.'

'And Papa's not here,' Eduardo adds, though it doesn't sound as happy as when I say it. Eduardo still loves Papa.

When we arrive at the creek a few minutes later, Eduardo runs over the bridge to get to the swings. I look down at the rocks and water running below. There's a pull in my belly as strong as the water falling down the hill.

'Chin up! Chin up! Gotta keep your chin up!' I mimic the hospice lady and her British accent, as I jump across the water.

Black plastic pots of four, six and eight wait for us along the north side of the house. He turns the packs of six upside down and wiggles the bottom of the pot back and forth, to loosen the bedding plant. It falls out into his hand and he shuffles to the end of the bed and starts to lean down.

'I'll get it.' From his hands, I take the baby plant and lay it on the soil.

He loosens another, and directs my hands to put it about a foot from the one on the left. We make windows with the second row, and again with the third row, so that every plant will have enough space. He sets a towel under his knees.

'Now we dig in, like this,' he pushes the trowel all the way into the soil, 'and pull back, and there's the hole.' He pulls the trowel out and hands it to me. All the soil has fallen back onto itself. 'Why don't you try the first one? We'll start with the back row.'

I push the tiny shovel in and pull back. Grandpa takes the little mini plant and places it in the space I've made. 'Now, let go.' I do and the dirt tumbles in around the plant. Grandpa spreads the soil to all the sides, explaining 'you gotta press it in, like this.' With his finger straight, he circles the stem and pushes the plant deep into the soil. 'Good, good, now this one.' I look down so Grandpa can't see me examine the veins on his left arm, pushing out. A huge one looks like a straw got stuck between his bones and skin. 'Why don't you try to plant this one?' When I press in around the stem, I watch Grandpa's eyes to see if I'm doing it right.

Every other morning I run out and water the tomato plants. Grandpa comes out the mornings he feels okay and watches. Once in a while we get a certain fertiliser and clip it onto the hose. When Grandpa gets tired, he sits on the picnic table and waits for me to finish. It's the same picnic table Grandpa and Great Uncle Lawrence are sitting on in all the photos we get sent every summer. Photos of the brothers, smiles that seem like they are getting harder to form, but their eyes always shine a bright blue. The photos make Mama laugh because most of them are of the garden: the cucumber and tomato plants, petunias and marigolds.

At night after we shower, we still get a story, but when Mama thinks Grandpa can handle it, she lets us ask him for one. Even though I am past the age for them, and Eduardo probably is too, we let him read us children's books like Dr Seuss and *Mad Dog*. His hands turn the pages slower, like the crank that churns him needs oil, but his voices are still wacky, and it's a relief to know that this part of him hasn't tired.

When Mama sees a picture of Grandpa playing on the carpet with our older brother when he was a toddler, she says 'maybe I should've had you younger, then you could've played with Grandma and Grandpa more.'

Mama is seeing another future I've never thought about. 'It's okay, Mama. We're getting to spend time with him now. That's important. This is a beautiful chance for you and me and Eduardo to show Grandpa how much we love him and spend his last summer with him.'

Mama cups my chin and starts to cry. 'How did you get to be so smart?' she asks, even though I am just repeating what she told me a month ago.

'Oh, it doesn't really matter.' He mumbles and starts shifting his feet back and forth, returning to the house. 'They're gonna die anyway.'

'What, Grandpa?' I ask, but I think I heard him. His mumbles get lost by the breeze, the creak of the door, the screen closing after him. The shock of the statement shoots the tears down fast. I drop the hose and run into the house, crying.

'I think I used the wrong fertiliser, or maybe I wasn't supposed to yet, I don't know. He just got mad I was doing it and said "they're gonna die anyway" and walked away.'

'He shouldn't have said that.' Her eyebrows are furrowed but something else is bothering Mama. Her gaze follows the stairs up to Grandpa's room.

'Is Grandpa mad at me? Do you think he doesn't love me now?' Her embrace is all around me, and my head is pushed into her skin around her clavicles.

'He's dying, sweetie.'

Light comes in, between the blinds and the air conditioner in the window.

'Dad, we love you so much. We're all here.'

'Bala, Eduardo and Andrew are here, and Share, Mary Ann and I are right here next to you.'

'You got your kids all around you, Dad. Your three beautiful, smart kids.'

'Thank you so much for all you've done for us, Dad. All the years you spent raising us, and taking care of us. Thank you for this summer with my kids.'

I look at Eduardo and his shoulders are shaking just like mine.

'Say hi to Mom for us!' Uncle Ed cries.

'We love you so much, Dad.'

'Mom's so happy to see ya, Dad.'

'We love you.'

The three adults keep reaching out, touching his hands, his head, his shoulders, kissing him, holding him, leaning in, then back, then leaning in again.

'We're gonna say goodbye, now, Dad.'

'Tell Mom we love her and we miss her so much.'

'We love you, Mom. Love you, Dad.'

Andrew is still crying quietly in the corner. His lips haven't parted the three days he and Aunt Mary Ann have been here. 'He was very close to Grandpa. You know they spent the whole summer here before the family moved to Alaska.' When I asked Mama why Andrew didn't talk she said, 'He's becoming a teenager. Boys stop talking for five years until they become adults.' I think of our older brother back home.

The official people come dressed in nurse clothes but they don't seem caring like the hospice lady.

Aunt Mary Ann whispers 'maybe the kids shouldn't watch, Sharon,' but Mama isn't looking at me or Eduardo. Her mind and attention are somewhere else, far away. The look on her face is terrifying in its unfamiliarity, like she is a different person than my mother, thoughts in her mind that aren't about me.

'One, two, three' and they swing Grandpa's body, not Grandpa, onto a cot, with a black bag open on it. They zip the body up quick and lift the cot out fast. I know why Aunt Mary Ann was worried, but it's really so easy to tell that Grandpa isn't there anymore, although I'm glad they are carrying the cot to the van with his old mouth right side up.

Metastasis

Bernie Crawford

i.m. Emer

A feather
and a bowling ball
drop together
in slow motion
in a vacuum.
Breath-taking,
but more beautiful than
their simultaneous fall
is the bounce
of the feather
when it lands.
It twirls in the air
displaying
the curved surface
of its vane
… except there is no air.
The bowling ball
bounces too
but not before it has
cracked open
the landing site.

Inside you
the feather
and the bowling ball
are dropping slowly.

To Answer Their Question

Anne Tannam

i
The dead are impatient with us
for our loss of imagination –
we who are
always leaving,

who daily step
blindfolded through
our field of vision,

we who swallow oceans,
we the unchartered

who roll a grain of sand
between finger
and thumb,
fashioning futures
in our own glass image,

we who understand
the sacred
mysteries of loss.

So why now, say the dead,
*why now this weeping,
this wringing of hands?*

ii
How little the dead remember
it's imagination that terrifies us most,
for in that theatre, loss plays
to an audience of one
over and over and over again –

a little boy wakens from a troubled
sleep,
sees his dead mother at the sink, calls
out to her;
and when this *almost* mother
turns around to face him,

her cheek is freshly bruised,
her upturned wrists newly slit.

The dead forget it's not the final scene
that paralyses us; it's the nightly return
to our seats, the mind rewinding,
the curtain rising.

Time

Emily Cullen

Your unassuming name gives you the false cast
of some perfectly affable chap, like Tom or Tim
with an extra vowel thrown in, yet you're the definition
of a creep, with a capital C; you stalk me when I sleep,
then steal precious hours when you insist that dawn
must break. How I've tried to get you on my side
since we first met as I left childhood behind, though
we were briefly on good terms when I parsed you
onto a paper plate with brass fastener, coloured
numbers, two cardboard hands; one long, one short.
I had every faith in my brand new friend. We shared
secrets then, about cherry blossoms, hidden nests with
speckled eggs, town spires prickling pink skies at dusk.

But you hung me out to dry when you caught me
short with errands, chores – even exams – undercut
by happenstance, with no redress to help me align
with your onward striding steps, just the demand
that I resign, again and again, to falling out of
sync as I carried over tasks on my swelling list.
I've since reconciled to the fact that you and I
will never see eye-to-eye, but at least I have
arrived at a place where I couldn't care less
for kinetic waves or the perennial hum of your
oscillating pendulum. Your seething seconds
no longer affect my outcomes. Instead,
I listen to the rhythm of my breath.

The Grind

Caroline Graham

I RING THE DOORBELL AND WAIT. Mulcahy's voice is bellowing around inside in the hall, shouting at some misfortune. That Lithuanian cleaner probably.

I glance over my shoulder. Still time to make a run for it. Down the path, jump the gate, round the corner and away. But where will that get me? No, got to keep the head. My one shot at making things right, I remind myself.

By the time she opens the door, her normal-person face is in place. Our eyes meet briefly on almost the same level.

'Come in, Darren.'

I step up into the hall and she shrinks back down to my shoulder level.

'That schoolbag of yours looks fierce heavy,' she says with a flurry of blinking behind her glasses.

'Yeah, just the books.'

'And just as well you're such a fine, strong fellow.' Off she goes with that screechy laugh of hers. My fists clench.

We go into her front room and I hand over Dad's money. She peeps inside the crumpled envelope before lodging it deep in her handbag. Upstairs the drone of the hoover kicks off. Dad always says she has it all worked out; my one-hour grind pays for three hours cleaning and the taxman's none the wiser.

As soon as we sit down, she starts. 'And how are you this week?' She's all smiles but I can see the hawkish look in the eyes. Circling, ready to pick at last week's sore. 'Feeling better?'

'Fine. Thanks.'

'That's great,' she says, but I sense her disappointment.

The room goes quiet. I flick a low glance in her direction. 'Just worried about my French exam.'

'I see.' She pauses long enough for a good gawk at me. 'Your oral is creeping up, so let's start with un peu de conversation.'

The last thing I need is more of what she calls conversation. Yet here she is with her 'Où habitez-vous?', as if I haven't already given her the dimensions of every room in our house, the colour of the en suite tiles, the name of my uncle's new girlfriend and the cost of the caterer for Izzy's communion. My heartbeat's beginning to rev up. I have to block her from going down the interrogation track again. But still I'm not ready to say my bit. Too early in the hour, I tell myself. 'Could you do some grammar with me instead, Miss?'

'Miss! What's with the Miss?' Her eyes are jigging around in her head, like she's all surprised. 'Didn't we agree you could call me Aideen during these lessons?'

'Yeah. Sorry. It's just I'm having difficulty with that subjunctive thing.'

'The sub-junc-tive?' She pronounces each syllable slowly, then waits as if the signal reception in her brain is on a break. 'Okay. If you need to focus on it for school.'

'Could you explain it in English? The rules, like. I can't figure them out.'

'You're not the only student to have problems with the subjunctive.' Then away she goes again as if she's cracked a real joke. I swear I'm allergic to that cackle of hers.

Off come the glasses and she begins polishing them with the corner of her cardigan. 'It's to do with wanting, wishing, obligation, necessity, doubt …' She's rhyming them off but I can see her eyes are connected to some other activity in her brain. And then the list trails off, the wire rectangles are in place again and I'm back under scrutiny.

'You seem very tense today, Darren.' She isn't going to let up.

Her hand creeps across to trap mine flat against the table. 'Remember what I told you when we had our little chat last week. You can always talk to me.'

I keep looking down at my books but I can feel her eyes drilling into me.

God, she gives me the shivers. What was I thinking of that last time? My cheeks burn with the memory. How could one stupid question in a torrent of others smash through all my defences? Qu'est-ce votre père a fait le weekend dernier? Any random answer would have done. Il a regardé la télévision or il est allé au match de rugby or some other old passé composé reliable. But no.

Even Mulcahy was caught unawares by my spectacular meltdown. She recovered well though. Out of the traps quickly with her questions. En anglais, of course, in case she'd miss anything. If it weren't for Jimmy Deasey arriving early for his own grind, who knows what other juicy details I might have fed her.

Having to face Mum's beaming face later that afternoon somehow made it worse. 'Guess who's inside in front of the TV? Go in and watch the match with him while I get the dinner on.' And not knowing where to park the memory of the afternoon's emotion as Dad grinned and slapped me on the shoulder. 'How's the man? How's that grind going? Still getting value out of that Mulcahy one? Can't have you wasting my good money, can we?'

Here I am, a week later, still fumbling to get my story right. How can I take back what I told Miss Mulcahy in confidence? Or the tears she witnessed? How can I tell the likes of her that Dad isn't such a bad guy? That Mum just overreacted, that he always intended coming home. A man needs a break once in a while.

I know I have to say something. My one chance. And there's still some hope, I remind myself. A good gulp of breath and I start. 'You remember that thing I told you last week ... about my dad?'

Her face lights up like a starving woman who's just been shown a plate of sizzling sausages. 'Of course I remember. I was so glad you felt you could confide in me.' It's all she can do to stop herself licking her lips.

'The thing is, it wasn't true.'

'Not true?' Her eyes withdraw into slits. 'What wasn't true?'

'I made it all up.'

'But you ...' She stops, puts her head to the side and smiles out the corner of her mouth. 'Ah, Darren, there's no need to be embarrassed.'

'I'm telling you, it was all lies.' My voice is high and wobbly but at least I've the tears still in check. 'I've been feeling terrible about it all week.'

'Lies?' She makes a clicky sound as she swallows. 'Are you sure?'

'Yeah. Certain. I'm really sorry, Miss. I don't know what got into me.'

I watch as her eyes flick around to various points in the room: the ceiling, the furry cushions, the photo of herself wrapped around some tosser in a Galway jersey. Her top teeth begin to scrape lipstick from the corners of her lower lip. First one side, then the other. The eyes return to meet mine with a hard, inescapable stare and with it comes the sharpness that's been missing from her voice for weeks. I know immediately I've seen the last of the call-me-Aideen personality.

'I'm absolutely shocked. What were you thinking of, Darren? What would your parents say if they knew what you said about them? It's bad enough telling me lies but did you even think of your father's reputation? Or what people would say about that Mrs Quinn?'

My silence is met by another volley. 'Have you any idea what a stupid thing you've done? The whole town could have this story by now. And it will be all your fault. Don't you realise that once you've told a lie, it's almost impossible to replace it with the truth?'

'But, Miss, you're the only person I told. And you promised it wouldn't go outside this room.'

For one brief moment, the power of my truth wobbles in the air. But as I try to match her long, silent glare, I find my eyes forced back down towards the books. I keep telling myself I have her snookered, but my heart refuses to listen. That blank stare tells me it's too late and I can only wonder how many have the inside story of our family.

My head is flooded with images of her salivating at each retelling: 'Sure the poor lad was so upset he couldn't control the tears.' I see them in huddles of two and three in kitchens around the town, in hairdressers, in Centra or up at the gym, flaunting their pretend sympathy while sharpening their long memories. Not one of them with Mum's tolerance for Dad's excuses. And it's only a matter of time before one big-mouthed parent ensures it goes viral in the school.

Miss Mulcahy's stare fades. She shrugs. 'I suggest we get back to the subjunctive.' She begins writing sentences on a sheet of paper, underlining words, pointing at them, her voice merging with the hoover.

All those fears that have haunted me for the last week elbow their way into my head again. Me sitting in the same classroom as Jason Quinn, knowing we're forever linked in every other lad's mind. Togging on and off in the same dressing room, the reason his mother is no longer at home like a bad stench hanging over us. Passing the ball to him at some crucial moment in a match, knowing full well what the real commentary will be. And Mum standing alone on the sideline, forcing herself to smile.

'Il est essential que; il est important que ...' The voice across the table suddenly breaks off from the shrill list. 'Are you listening to me, Darren?'

But my attention is fixed on the short path outside the window, dreading what lies beyond it and praying for Jimmy Deasey to arrive early.

To a Friend Who is Sad and Far Away

Deborah Bacharach

Imagine I am bringing you raspberries, fresh picked
the perfume snuggling around corners
under doorways, sweet heady, already with you
before you even have a chance to open the door
to deep jewel tones. Imagine each gift
on your tongue, abundant.

Imagine the scaffolding did not collapse, your colleagues
agreed with your plan, the judge ruled in your favour.
Imagine you won a Fulbright, the diagnosis wrong,
your daughter allowed
to live with you the rest of your days.
Imagine the man you loved, loved you.

Then imagine me in the rows of raspberry canes
I shuffle leaves, turn my body upside down
to find the still ripe.
I tender lift each glow from the vine
where it has grown because
of how the earth moves, how the sun
leans in and someone's great care.
Imagine I am thinking of you.
Know that this is true.

Two Deaths

Michael Brown

after Otzi

and sometime to be carried like a spore
above the snowline of a life. Brought
to light by hands that had never touched you,
unclothed the mystery of a body.
Here to know what it is to die alone,
they dress what's left of your papery skin
with their strange forensic tenderness.
To them the circumstances of death are unknown,
they make an educated guess,

determine next of kin, contact
wife, care home.
And, yes, they'll wonder at the colour of your hair,
the precise contents of your final meal,
a time shown on a receipt found
near the scene somewhere,
the last thirty-six hours and more:
what you were running from and to,
exactly what it was that led you here.

Unearthed

Edel Burke

What favours did the ancients seek
when they laid bones in a boulder chamber

amidst moss and sedge, took
the long trudge up and down Bengorm

walked across heather and turf hags,
through boggy, grassy slopes?

When they placed pieces of quartz
among the bones, they couldn't have known

the secrets, how its crystals keep time,
resonate to transmit frequencies

we now call radio, television.
They must have known

how its translucence can charm light,
attune to the force of the universe,

a pull between rock and moon.
Was it afterlife they sought, the soul's release?

And as for the placing of bones,
undiscovered for five thousand years,

even with all we now know,
there are still things this earth withholds.

Percussion

Laura Treacy Bentley

In those long winters of unending snow,
the coal furnace rattled from the cellar,
the radiators clanged,

and a stained-glass window
shivered in its azure-blue skin.

Seven children were born and loved

in this storied brick home
where, in her final years,
their stone-deaf grandmother

lay bedfast faraway upstairs.
She drummed the floor with a wooden cane

until her raven-haired granddaughter

climbed the winding stairs and appeared
with a hot cup of green tea,
stirred with warm milk and two sugars.

But the tea was cold
and would never do,

so Mary poured it out

and stomped down to the kitchen
where a fresh cup was brewed.
She carried it, much faster now,

up each creaky flight – two steps at a time –
never spilling a single drop

as the furnace rumbled,

the radiators ticked and groaned,
and every pane frosted over
while grandmother's cane

beat the floor like a crazed metronome
until stoic Mary

stepped out of time.

Ireland's Eye

Dylan Brennan

The northern gannets, black-and-white razorbills
damp ferns, creamy speckle of cow-parsnip
that unexpected carpet of large daisies
that led us to the summit with our sandwiches –
Lily, my brothers, a friend who'd lost his mother
– where we ate and passed around my hip flask
single malt whiskey and the sun-dried tomatoes
salted on our tongues by the easterly seaspray

I take down from my Mexico City shelf
a glass jar that used to contain mustard and pour
onto the table what I took from that island
what Simon scooped into a old crisp packet
– microscopic fan shell upon sand and pebbles
and what I think is the vertebra of a fish
taken cold from the Irish Sea and dashed on rocks
– a matte organic little puck that sits on top

Every time I do this, every time I brush it
all back into the jar I leave
in the flexion creases of my palm
some traces behind
some crushed saltiness of motherland

The Middle of the Night, A Dark Hallway

John Higgins

MAYBE IT'S BECAUSE YOU HAVE ALWAYS been convinced that you're special. That you were brought onto this earth for a purpose. That you will be the best in the world at something. That you have something to offer. That you have unrealised potential. That you haven't written your novel yet. Or composed a concerto. Or won an Oscar. Or cured cancer. Or discovered a new constellation. Or found true love.

Maybe that's why you accept the lift without hesitation.

You're glad just to be off your feet. The burning sensation prickling your soles vanishes the moment you slide into the passenger seat. You retract your thumb. You notice how sore it is from jutting out at passing cars for hours.

The car smells of car. The pine air-freshener dangling from the mirror. Old cigarette butts crippled in the dashboard ashtray. Dust in the upholstery tickling your nose. A grease-sodden fast-food bag crumpled up in the back seat. A bag of tools beside it. The stench of dried sweat, lying beneath all this like white noise.

There's a radio but it's not playing. The silence is eerie. The driver breathes like they've called a late-night sex chatline. The silence is encroaching. The silence is unbearable.

You say thanks for this. You say it clearly. You enunciate every syllable. You ensure that the kind benefactor who has picked you up is aware of your gratitude.

You ask where they're going. They don't respond. A feeling: dry-mouthed unease. You quash it down. You tell them where you're going. It's far. You point anyway. As though it's just up here on the left.

The comforting golden arches of a McDonald's appears. You see through the windows. You see the gaudy colours. You see the white counter. You see the brims of logo'ed caps. You see a family. You see a man eating a double cheeseburger by himself. Then it's gone.

You try to relax. You tell yourself that it's fine. You tell yourself that the driver is just one of those oddballs. An outcast with little in the way of social graces. You charitably blame anxiety for your saviour's withdrawn nature.

You look at the driver. They look perfectly ordinary. Their side-profile doesn't speak of aberrance.

You try your best to ignore the intensity with which they're watching the road. You fail. You remind yourself of others' little idiosyncrasies. You remind yourself how an uncle doesn't speak while driving. How your mother cannot stand the radio playing while driving. You lay a blanket of respectability over all of this. You make associations with the real world that calm your quickening heartbeat.

You look back and the rest stop is a distant memory. It may never have existed. The man with the cheeseburger, the lonely cars parked up outside, the family dipping nuggets into pots of sauce. You will never see them again.

You blame yourself.

You hear the dull thud of the locks engaging and you blame yourself. You watch the last of civilisation flit by the passenger window. You watch the lights, the houses, the windows, the porches, the disused barbecues. The Ford Mondeos, the recycling bins, the fences, the rusted bicycles.

You watch all these things be replaced by trees. Massive trees, either side of the road, rising from the centre of the earth and piercing the sky.

You don't know the names of different trees. You can't distinguish them. You call fir trees Christmas trees. These trees, jutting out of the earth, knitting themselves across the heart of the forest so you can only see leaves and blackness, are unknown to you.

You tell the driver that they can let you out anywhere soon. You say you're meeting someone around here. You know it's a pathetic excuse but fear has clouded your brain.

Still, you don't let the threat of your death make an embarrassment of you. You refrain from making a scene. Manners cost nothing, after all.

You politely ask the driver to stop. They ignore you. The car is building speed, slicing along the empty road that cleaves the forest in two. The trees slide by faster and faster, the world around you a mere blur. A car passes and you bang on the window. You hear the sudden screech of brakes as the car does a U-turn. You hear the sirens of police cars coming over the precipice of the road. It's all your imagination, of course. You see the last red glint of the car's brakelights heading towards the McDonald's however far back.

Your fear of causing a scene dissipates as the driver slowly tilts the steering wheel and the car falls from the tarmac onto a dirt road, the conical headlight beams catching the brick-red dust that is thrown up by the approaching tyres.

You try the door even though it's locked, the handle snapping closed impotently. You hit the button that controls the windows but they've locked that too, from the dimly lit command centre. You try to break the window but it's useless. You hammer on it, the tempered glass shaking promisingly in its rubber frame, and then nothing. The car continues, you give up, your palm tingling with pain.

You toy with the idea of grabbing the wheel, attacking the driver, but your fear of certain death is stronger than your fear of abstract death. You can already see it: the claustrophobic scuffle; the dull feeling of some previously concealed blade piercing your abdomen, puncturing some major organ; the sudden jerk as the car lifts into the air, twisting and ploughing directly into a tree; the blackness of the forest bursting into life as the car explodes outward like a sun.

You look out the window, the scenery cast into a darkness that is so foreboding you can viscerally imagine deformed bodies racing from the forest towards the car, you can imagine hands shooting out of shallow graves, you can imagine a glint of demonic red in the face of the driver, their eyes still fixed on the road, panting heavier and heavier as they navigate the forest path.

You don't know how it can be this, your ultimate end coming in some abandoned log cabin, or maybe just a clearing between the trees. You imagine the feel of dirt in your mouth, cable-ties biting into your wrists, the sound of the boot slamming closed and the scrape of a shovel coming closer, closer.

You were destined for something greater than this surely, you think, your heart pounding like a revving engine before the clutch is released, or bucking like a horse in the traps. You were destined for something greater than this, the words flit through your mind like neon mockeries, words that would have ordinarily caused you embarrassment.

Your mother or father, maybe a teacher or professor here or there, a supervisor or manager, sometimes just a friend taking you aside as you hit your rock-bottom, told you that you were better than *this*, and *this*, whatever *this* has been, has been transformed into *this*, every moment marked off by the air-freshener pendulum ticking back and forth, back and forth, as the car slowly winds its way through the woods, the last signs of humanity – tarmac, cat's-eyes, families enjoying Happy Meals, the sudden burst of dazzling headlights strafing across your eyes – now finally gone, as though by merely leaving the road you and your captor have somehow travelled in time, back to some Palaeolithic era, you and the driver the only two sentient beings on earth.

The driver is slowly losing their cool, their knuckles white as your face, their fingers hooked over the steering wheel's spokes. They mutter to themselves, but it's so low you can't make out any of it. Nor, in a sense, do you want to, clinging to the infantile hope that should have left you four or five kilometres back, that the driver is merely debating whether to let you free here or carry you to some Burger King rest stop at the other end of the forest.

So you continue, you and your driver, into the forest, all the while ruminating on the unfairness of it all, when you compare your potential with that of any other person who could have been picked up today, slaughtered; becoming some statistic, remaining a footnote in the historiography of the driver, a simple blue hyperlink on your killer's Wikipedia page that no one ever clicks on because, after all, no one reads about the victim, do they? and knowing your current fortune, the change in your existence's dynamic, you know you probably don't even have the privilege of being the first, or the last: you'll be somewhere around the middle, the memorable names bookending yours in their uniqueness, while you remain, forever, victim #4, #6, #11, some unremarkable number, your death serving only to accentuate the interest in your killer, your driver, and the car starts to slow, finally, and the headlights alight upon a clearing, some rotunda embedded in the heart of the forest, a space where no one can hear you scream.

The Seventeenth of May

Fiona B. Smith

THE THAW WAS ALL THE SWEETER for coming late to Viksdalen. The drip drop drip of that first, crucial portent of spring set the village's life blood pumping. The river, transfused, turned red for joy and began to course again. At the sight of the first crocus, the Alpine saxifrage, the villagers cleared the silage mulch of leftover snow, examined their richly embroidered national costumes, dusted them down, deemed them fit and came mad alive.

Gyrid was the first to suggest they formed a committee for the Seventeenth of May, their constitution day. It was the same every year. The same members, the same procedures and she was always the one to initiate it. Nonetheless, she refused to take on a role more important than treasurer and committee member. Although repeatedly offered the chair, she always said, 'I'll leave that to the mayor.'

At lengthy evening meetings twice a week, they planned the parade. They fussed over it.

'What if the weather is bad?' They fought over who would lead it. Gyrid favoured the mayor, such a handsome, imposing figure in his Viksdalen *bunad*, but there were those who argued for the doctor or the rector. The mayor stayed silent throughout, knowing that the offices of the state would prevail as always. They deliberated over what they should bake. There had been too much *white lady* last year, so easy to make, with the more exacting marble cake overlooked. Much time was spent on the question of who would be invited to come to see their mountain – *Gaulafjellet* – transformed from white to greenish blue. Preferably, a returned famous son or daughter, but these were running out. Many former residents, having found success on the national stage, preferred Oslo for the national day. They appeared to have little time or interest in celebrating the seventeenth on the street down which villagers in their patriotic best had marched with trumpets, pipes and horns since 1814.

The seventeenth of May heralded the start of a long, and often hot, summer. A season during which it seemed to the villagers – on that day, at least – that anything might happen.

The butcher blinked himself awake and scurried to his store. A couple of beers after last night's football match had left the world bleary and unfocussed. The beer had been in the company of his friend Mikhael, a Kosovan farm worker who helped him out part-time. He regretted that he had spent most of the evening complaining about his ex. A wave of hot, alcohol-sweat shame came over him. Mikhael wouldn't mind, he self-soothed. 'He had women problems of his own. Next time, his turn.'

This morning again he was pondering the personal when his mind should have been on sausages. The supply of sausages would have to be steady. For the children there would be sausages before the parade. During the parade, there would have to be sausages for those whose age, infirmity or cussedness ensured they would not take part. After the parade people would need the sustenance of a sausage or two. The seventeenth of May was the most profitable day of the entire year. Besides, Jarle considered sausage supply to be an essential public service. Civic-minded, he had thrown the school sausages in for free. He had been working hard for weeks on end to make sure of his sausage supply. Surely his devotion to work had not been why his wife had left? He had to make a living after all. But meat was not glamorous. Her new paramour worked in the city. Sharp-suited, gym-toned. He had a big boat. Investments.

White teeth. Best not dwell on it when he was up to his oxters in sausage meat and besides, he would have Anna back this evening. He would be bound to run into Annette, the beautician, with her son.

Gyrid looked down from her hill-top eeyrie. She had time to kill. Her pristine house was cleaner than it had ever been. She had delivered her baking to the school the night before. She looked down at the house of the beautician whom she deemed flighty. Nothing.

She must have already left for the school. Then Jarle the butcher caught her eye as he sweated the sausages in his shop. 'Not good for a man to be alone.'

Annette was not looking forward to the day. The best efforts of the early morning bugler, signalling the dawn of their constitution day, had done nothing to lift her spirits. Her mood had not been improved by another light night in front of the TV alone. She had ignored her alarm clock three times, rising at the last minute for the revels. 'Time to get up,' she yelled and hauled her son's cornet downstairs and placed it by the door.

'Come down,' she bellowed at Jonas, 'we'll be late for the parade.'

After breakfast she spent five minutes under the white lights of her bathroom repairing the damage of yet another sleepless night. Her contrivances, she hoped, had fixed her face into a convincing rictus to greet the proud parade-going mothers at the school hall.

'Mamma, I can't wait for the sausages,' yelled Jonas. 'Then I can have an ice cream after the parade, can't I?'

'Of course you can, darling.'

Hard to believe he was nearly twelve. It was good to see him excited. The school band had been good for him. Band practice had given him something to do in this quiet village where if you didn't like football you were worse than nothing. At the hall the band was tuning up, faces in instruments gleaming. The band looked its best, uniforms pressed, best bib and tuckered.

'O the tedium of it,' she thought, but did not say.

Annette longed for witty men with whom to mix *double entendres* and vodka. Men who would flirt, and flirt – especially with her. No, only with her and with her alone. She longed to be the centre of attention, a specific type of attention.

She wandered off to get a coffee, declining to hang around the hall with the other mothers. She would be watching when Jonas walked down the street with his cornet. That would be enough. She stopped near the sausage stall to look for a spot to await the merry marchers.

Her beautiful skin was forked between the eyes as she mulled the privations of living in the Norwegian countryside with farmers' wives for clients. The sausage-laden air hit her powdered nose.

'Disgusting,' she thought.

She wished she could be in Oslo to lunch at the Teater cafe – lobster with a drop of cold, white wine would be nice. Instead the penury precipitated by divorce and the high rents of Oslo had forced an unscheduled return to her childhood home, her inheritance and her scourge. She positioned herself beside the doctor and his wife. She barely knew them. They would not expect any conversation from her besides an easy pleasantry.

'Cold wind, isn't it?'

The doctor smiled. Indeed, it was unseasonably cold that May 17th. The bitter wind that blew from the mountains across the icy lake beyond the graveyard would have consequences for his patients. Or at least those inclined to catch a chill. These were his chronic, heart-sink patients for whom May 17 was not a diversion. Instead they saw it as a lost opportunity, a closed day which forced them to refrain from the near-daily relish of their visits to the doctor's office. His office was their refuge and their sanctuary where he heard their ailments with unfailing courtesy and patience. Not one suspected that placid, kindly Doktor Johansen while appearing to listen to their symptoms was adding ever richer detail to the escape fantasy that played a central part in the drama of his inner life. For as his wife planned their retirement comfort in a cosy cabin, the doctor dreamed of running away to the Canaries with the beautician, whose rude good health meant she had never once entered his office.

Instead she spent time in his imagination, where she was destined to remain. Most of his adult life he had been a family man – prudent, solvent. Yet recently, he had arrived at a time of disquiet, a questioning of the retriever-like obedience of what had gone before. He felt that this should be his time. His friend Alf had travelled east.

Thailand had produced any number of brides for Norwegian men. There would be no need to advertise. A solo holiday would suffice. He had quite a bit put by. His wife – Merete – 'Happy 17th elskling' need not suffer, nor be put out financially, or in any other way. He might have to prepare the ground after their nightly game of Yahtzee. He might mention that he and some old school friends were thinking of a men's holiday away.

The stall was perfectly placed for those pining for warmth. The early sunshine was deceiving and winter's chill had not quite finished testing Viksdalen's stoicism.

Gyrid took her best tweed coat and made for Main Street where the villagers were cheering on the marchers. Uttering 'oohs' and 'aahs', they feigned more than they felt. Gyrid stood to admire the children, fluttering blue, white and red as the band struck up at the end of the street. With their ornate costumes of green and gold embroidered, their curlicued instruments, you'd swear you were in Hamlyn. Down the main street they marched, past the Joker grocery shop, the petrol station, the coloured swings and kindergarten slides.

As the band pumped out the proud refrain, 'Ja vi elsker dette landet', the marchers stopped at Bell's shop to wave, then turned on their collective heel.

Then they passed the sausage stand, where beautician and butcher stood, Annette's expertly powdered cheek by Jarle's flushed jowl. A look between the honest sausage seller and the beautician was not lost on Gyrid, transfixed by the smell of sausage meat and potential sex. A union between butcher and beautician – if not illicit – would add some spice to May the seventeenth.

As Annette watched the marchers coming down the street, she put out her delicate, freshly manicured hand. She turned in Jarle's direction, noted his white-apronned eagerness. She considered him a moment. Tried to imagine it. Then dismissed the thought.

A good guy, but 'not my type, too fleshy'.

The seventeenth of May fairytale was not to be. Gyrid went home frustrated. Annette left to spend the evening with her dreams of Oslo and her surround sound.

A querulous Jarle took down his stall. Maria's presence denied him the opportunity to brood on his former wife's good fortune, her partner's permatan. They ate ice cream and watched a video together, *Frozen 2*. She liked the second one best. Every now and then she checked her new phone, a birthday present from her mother and her new beau. Jarle had not been pleased about it but there was nothing he could do.

'Can Jonas come over tomorrow?' Maria asked.

Her father started from his couch slumber. He smiled.

'Oh, yes, of course he can, tell him to ask his mum to drop him over and I will drop him home.'

Holidays

Iain Twiddy

Norfolk now, our summer holidays gone,
but especially the first one: the window open
to the evening stream slowly reeding its way

down to days dazed by sun, dazzling marram,
blustering blue on the tops of the dunes,
plump leaps into a hot bath of sand.

Sandwiches, oh, so they must come from the beach.
Eggshell and sea shells, worms that were wet sand,
scattered razors that could slice off a foot.

And clearly, her feet, bare in brown sandals,
Mary then, Aphrodite, Athene now,
walking me down to the water, the voice

mouthing, erasing again, its own shape,
the creamy foam sizzling like rattled snakes,
then the cold knuckling the toes, clutching the ankles,

licking the calves and thighs like a million
melting ice lollies, the blubby upswell
sucking back to the bulk, to that heaving

blue whale that could swallow me like Jonah,
until she lifted me into orbit, in water,
held me abrim between heaven and earth.

All gone now, this morning, all gone, it's clear,
the tide of night dragged back to another
mass stranding, another memory pod

swept from the brain's foam-strewn waves, not even
a candle-gutter of recognition,
a pilot light like a whale's tiny eye

in all that expanse of terrified whale,
all irrevocably gone from an ocean
they once as serenely inhabited

as I did another swelling, unbroken globe.

Quarantine II

Kate Quigley

I text the man next door
whose name I don't know,
his fat little dog
screams at me through
the cardboarded windows
when I step onto the driveway –
brown bread on your wheelie bin,
hope all good with you.
I don't want any credit for this.
Only for something to rise
from my hands,
small organic chemistry of
bicarb, buttermilk.
Fermentation is a type of growth.
Every evening the local cats come,
the grey, the ginger,
sit on the wall between our houses
stare into the lush jungle of weed
wait for something to twitch.

Scapegoats

Peter Branson

Floral tributes have been left where the body of a rough sleeper was found near the Central Museum and Art Gallery in Hanley, Stoke-on-Trent. One homeless charity claimed the man was attacked by three thugs and struck in the face with a hammer days before he died. Lindow Man, also known affectionately as Pete Marsh, is a preserved bog body discovered near Wilmslow, Cheshire, on 1st August 1984 by commercial peat-cutters.

To my good friend John Beech

Pete Marsh was overkilled like you, his head
stoved in, garrotted, throat slashed, bled, then drowned,
the mangled, marrow-less remains, like creased,
discarded leathers in a barn, outweighed
by sods, intact, adulterer or thief,
prisoner of war or murderer perhaps,
or witting sacrifice to sooth false gods,
conserved and chronicled behind plate glass.
Your death was brewed by local youths who struck
you with a hammer on both cheeks. You froze
here three days later like a worn jute sack,
your middle-aged rough sleep exposed, where folk
who cared at last laid flowers, your epitaph
Since Last Year, Nothing's Changed! yesterday's news.

A Season of Picking Up

Lynn Caldwell

Someday someone will trace their finger
over the stubby scar
under his chin
and ask *How?*
maybe he will tell
of the smooth skate park, his scooter
and one last hurrah of a hot August evening

He slipped

> the blood hot, fast
> crimson
> not nearly as shocking
> as his howls.

His grandfather fell under the apple tree
picking up windfalls
that week too
his breath quieter, his calls
near inaudible
long minutes before we saw him
the ground summer-dry

it took two of us to help him stand,
dark spots already appearing
on the apples, scattered.

It was a season of picking up
putting back together.

The scars are small
unseen except by lovers.

Simply Meeting for Coffee

Frank Dullaghan

To be close,
the gift of shared silences,
coffee flavouring the tongue,

sun slanting from the window,
sharpening the edge of the table,
staining the floor,

the self, losing itself,
content to float,
that irresistible urge to smile,

moments that forget
the body, the mind marinating
in a slow enjoyment.

Life is filled with noise.
But there is space
if you make space.

Bully #6

Rory Duffy

Blue haemorrhaged ink,
your homework pages
in the pitted rain.

A gutted inner tube
on your lacerated,
dead birthday bike.

Dog shit school bag,
could do better, letters,
your mam's blue cigarette breath.

A new unpleasant tang,
the taste for beer and twice,
those midnight river eyes.

A mother's goodbye,
your plastic passport stare,
that Wembley carpet bed.

The drip-drip boredom,
of security guard nights
and weekend barman nods.

Can of strong lager.
Christmas Eve.
Central line,
alone.

Garden Shed

Cian Ferriter

Through the shed's squat door,
I am back to a tower block
in East Berlin before the fall

where every night at ten
the State-employed caretaker
with the B-movie limp

locked our flat door from the outside
and where, at midnight,
the man in the flat above

dropped empty beer bottles
onto the concrete plaza below,
glass exploding as he roared

expressions in old German
(consisting, we learned later, of a series
of agricultural curses

directed largely at his mother);
our door unlocked again at dawn
although by whom, we never saw.

Cursing Stone

Billy Fenton

On the boat to Caher Island, the boatman said:
You turn it over and recite your curse.

I think of the customs ship that sank
off Tory Island, killing fifty-two, after the locals

used their stone to plant a curse. I smile to myself,
bemused by what men can believe.

In the falling church of Patrick, on a makeshift altar,
between a bullaun of water and a pile of rusting coins,

a brightly coloured conglomerate stone,
smoothed into roundness by the churn of the sea.

I touch its coldness. Afraid to turn it over.
Afraid to pretend ill words. I hesitate

at the doorway. Tempted to return to show
what can't be true. Outside, the wind is shivering.

Sea speckled with broken bread. Patrick's Mountain
pyramids its fingers into a razor grey sky,

calls out a prayer to an unseen God.
Above the beach three gulls tear a lamb to pieces.

The Sin Collector

David C. Hall

The sin collector comes in
about half past nine,
or maybe half past ten,
in his scruffy wool coat,
bag over his shoulder
and sparse lank hair.

Eyes not as scary as you might think
but rather soft and weepy, wet,
like fried eggs just before they fry,
a drip of snot on his unshaven lip.

Evening, nice weather, bit cold,
he mumbles, head down
as he makes the rounds,
holding open the bag's dark mouth.
We drop in what we've got.
We never look inside.

An icy breath blows in from the night
and then he's out the door and gone.
I wonder where he goes with that,
somebody says, as he picks up his glass.

I lift my lighter out of the beer slop
on the bar and thumb the wheel
that flicks the flame to life,
and I imagine the street as he trudges along,
ice on the puddles, the rattle of the wind.

For the One Who Has Lived Too Little and Too Long

Kevin Higgins

after George Hitchcock

I wait for the ruin inherent in every building
to emerge triumphant;
I wait for the eight foot tall woman to stop dancing
around my mind with her three foot tall man;
I wait for the blood test that might be the beginning of a solution.

I wait for the recently widowed magpie
to alight brutally on the garden fence;
I wait for the handcuffs and laxatives;
I wait for the doctor to try not to frown
and choose her words very carefully.

I wait for this particular mouse-trap
to embrace its prey in its jaws;
I wait for the Sanity Protection Office
to respond to my letter about the world's failure
to stop reminding me you're still in it;

I wait for the car alarms to not let you sleep
and the morphine to not quite work;
I wait for the skeleton to be set free from its flesh.

I wait for the kidneys and heart
to be sold to a buyer in, we think, Tajikistan;
I wait for the bed sheets and mattress
to be taken out and burnt;
I wait for the specially extended
extra long coffin I've been
ecstatically hammering together
to envelope and take you away.

Skins

Fiona Nic Dhonnacha

MY FINGERS TREMBLE AS I QUICKLY ROLL tobacco flakes between the smooth paper trench and use the tip of my tongue to seal it into a perfect cylindrical cigarette. It's a skill I'm proud of, mastered over years of manure-scented sessions in neighbours' fields where I impressed all the boys. As I got older, I could roll a perfect cigarette – or a joint – with one hand at dense, sweaty parties, even when I could hardly see straight from the alcohol swilling through my veins.

I spark up. There are a few of us pale-faced rebels out here, ignoring the droning nosmokingonhospitalgrounds playing on repeat. I inhale nice and deep and imagine the smoke curling into my lungs, blood cells trooping through millions of air sacs working to get oxygen to my heart, diaphragm squeezing and expanding like an umbrella. In sixth class we watched a video about how smoking turns your lungs shrivelled and black. I pulled at the webbed skin between my fingers under my desk as I watched in absolute horror. I went home with a stomach cramp, begging my mother to quit as she tapped ash into a saucer at the kitchen table. 'Ar toil Dé chuile shórt,' she said solemnly, a classic scapegoat answer. I cried for three nights straight. Two years later I was spending lunchtimes lounging behind the school, puffing Silk Cut purple with swagger.

I toss the butt and tuck the lighter into my pocket. My mother stopped smoking not long after she got cancer but it had grabbed hold savagely, and she deteriorated fast as it tore strips at her insides. Before my eyes she morphed into a strange, sickly caricature. When I was really small, I would sit on her lap while she drank her morning coffee and perform manoeuvrings on her soft, doughy features. I would gently pinch the soft folds of her face, fascinated by how flesh would sink slowly back into place while my own chubby cheeks sprang like an elastic. I marvelled at the engrained lines around her eyes, the vertical grooves in between her eyebrows.

After she got sick her cheeks became hollow and sunken, like a scoop had taken a chunk right out of her and just left the bone, impossibly sharp; it looked ready to snap out of her skin if she smiled too hard. Over time, her skin draped loosely over her bones like an old dress she couldn't really wear anymore. Yet it hung obstinately as she shrunk smaller and smaller inside its folds.

I check my watch – I've been here six hours now – and paw at my chest to feel the thumpthumpthump of my heart. I feel for the bones in my wrists, the reassuring mounds standing to attention out of my skin.

OK, focus. Get back inside. Automatic doors yawn open, pump the sanitiser twice, through the second set of doors. In the soapy melodrama of my mother's cancer, we're at the tissue-wringing part where everyone gathers around the bedside for hushed reminiscences and mumbled prayers.

I'm years playing dutiful daughter, but my heart still starts kicking every time I come back here. Sweat gathers in my collarbone and trickles slowly down, coating my chest in a slippery glaze. I think about how our bodies pump and circulate and secrete and expand and contract until it all starts breaking down, whether it's age or bad luck or poison of choice. My uncle died two years before my mother's diagnosis. His liver soaked up alcohol like an old sponge until it couldn't hold any more and forty years' worth of whiskey leaked through the pores and drowned him.

My bones clack together, grinding and heavy with dread as I walk slowly towards her room. My chest feels hot and there's something prickly lurking in my ribcage, threatening to attach itself to my lungs. I can hear the blood roaring in my ears and my whole body hums with adrenaline as I keep moving forward, towards the doors and my mother and her face and her sickness. Maybe she's still there, filling the space with her last sputtering breaths. Maybe she is already gone. Sloughed out of her body, a snake finally shedding its old skin.

Reading the Runes

John D. Kelly

Don't think too much
    within the sweet flow
of one-way streets
    or its arrowed signs
might lead you
        to a place
where the missed marks
of an archer's sins
will fade like weak words,
    not heady runes,
hoisted on posts
like pikes;

or where the potent tip
of a Sky-God's spear
gets battered into
a dark 'T' and presents
a stark choice

of only *sinister*   or right;

or, if more lucky, it'll be
beaten and tempered
    after the fire of forging
into the sweet gentle 'Y'
of a road that's
        only diverging;

or, worst of all,
    you might find yourself
in the never-ending bend
    of an already well-rutted
poetic 'O'
and you too might go
    round and round all day
repeating, repeating . . .
        repeating.

No Answers

Gerard Smyth

(On returning to my old school 50 years later)

They blend into memory,
the school desk with the inkwell, the black soutane,
my friend, the butcher's son humming *Let's Twist Again*.
In those days the side gate was opened at three o'clock
and we went running into afternoon sun or blowing rain.

I returned again to that childhood school,
saw my name inscribed on a page
from the year Gagarin became the first man in space
while here on earth prayers were offered
for those on the wrong side of the Berlin Wall.

The ledger had names in Gaelic form but the faces
they should have prompted were too faded to dredge from memory.
And after the classroom song and welcoming ceremony
when I saw those hands in the air
I remembered there are questions I have no answer for.

Trees Begin to Loosen

Mercedes Lawry

Polar bodies hold no secrets.
What becomes debris is not calculated
but borne on a weak wind or trickling stream.
As those who scour alleys
and damp closets, discarded boxes
and the bones settled by the back shed,
conceal their true desires. Flakes of sin
trail from the confessional in the sour
lamplight of a January afternoon.
Imagine wisdom as commonality, influence
as cipher, the bold blue of a north sea
laid with the trimmings of smoky light.
The eye of science roams the mess
in search of patterns and reason,
while rivers rise in a waiting game
and trees begin to loosen from the earth.

Bright May Morning

Patrick Kehoe

I will walk – having taken some train or other –
among the homely glass and steel towers
Of the Ensanche, resigned to the upheaval
Of uptown emptiness, as though the vendors
Sold newspapers without print, or hollow things
In cellophane, scratched their heads
And tried to remember us, until the bright May morning

And its lively seance offered a clue
As to who we were, where we were, what we were,
Long before flowers became efflorescence,
Or blue became azure, twilight crepuscular,
All those needless words occluding the memory.

The Housewife's Ars Poetica

Adina Kopinsky

after Kelly Grace Thomas

I write a poem with the edges of the mop on the floor / with soap suds in the kitchen sink, I write a poem / in the smudges of the window, in the frost of the car / I write a poem in voice-to-text when I cannot / find a pen / Greek: *poema*, a thing made / restructured / slashed through with possibility

I write a poem in my lap as I drive, I write a poem / with the gas nozzle as I fill up my car; I write / a poem in the dirt, in the piles of leaves, in pebbles at the park / repurpose each bit of organic matter / into its own pod of string / weave of tears

I write a poem on the backs of shopping lists / on my son's homework, on his health card / in the creases of his bedsheet; I write a poem in wax / in finger paint, in honey on bread / the house is graffitied / with my words, the children sleep on pillows / stuffed with drafts; I write a poem with spaghetti / and feed it to them letter by letter

I carve *poesis* on the collar / of a goat named Azazel / watch as he is pushed off a cliff / to atone for delirium / I use sand to shape a poem / affix each speck in glue / the grains condensing / into the form of an hourglass

Like a one-woman chorus / of ancient tragedy – *tragodia,* / or 'goat song'. I sing, / in Hebrew *shir* / one word; both poem and voice / timbre, tambourine, the rhythm / of the waves' libation / the grit of life bespoke for me, I speak / for it / my tuneless voice transcribing the shifting plates / plastic, tectonic

In my head a hysteria / of hope / from Latin 'womb', dysfunction of the uterus / me, ink running out of orifices, appendages / turning to pen beneath the pain / of creation squeezed *ex nihilo* / into nothing / out of earth into earth / out of heart into heat / of day, out of mother / into child / out of woman into world

Last Night

Rachel Morton

Last night I slept and dreamt of singing moths.
Of daffodils drumming in this Lent air.
I dreamed of stillness.
Of peace stretching out
in the six directions and beyond.
It was a deep and heavy sleep,
anchoring my flying mind.
I dreamed of filling huge water containers
in a terrible thirst
after a long walk in the bush.
And I woke to no water in the taps,
wishing I had filled containers
in this waking life as well.
I dreamed rolling images
of people and their happiness.
So much happiness,
it spilled out into the street.
Their lives were filled with polka-dot dresses.
Their walking was almost dancing.
Their smiles were wide.
They were never alone.
If they were not with friends,
they were surrounded by family.

They walked, on sunny Sunday mornings,
to city cafes, where they had brunch.
But, at the end of the day,
when the cameras were off,
and they were alone in their rooms,
they could not hold back the tears.
They peeled off their false eyelashes,
washed away their glittery make-up.
And for reasons I did not understand,
alone, in the dark, they
took a photograph
of their grief.

From Montdevergues Asylum

Úna Ní Cheallaigh

after the letters of Camille Claudel

As if there were no words,
just cold white marble pressed against palms;

as if you wanted to say we clasp this secret,
like the unborn child we never held;

as if our fingertips barely touching
showed what passed between us;

as if the clay of Montfavet would be enough
to make me nameless.

*

Times when it's so hard I cannot bear it –

I rub stale bread between my fingers,
feel the curve of cold tin plates,

my hands longing for clay to mould the pain,
to cast their vacant eyes, their bitten nails.

I gave my hands, my young body to Rodin,
you'll find them burning at *The Gates of Hell*.

Sculptor Camille Claudel *(1864–1943)*
The Secret and The Gates of Hell, works by sculptor Auguste Rodin *(1840–1917)*

Wasps

Rachel Parry

whenever the sun dropped
its blanket of light
over the willow bower
the air filled with a high
whine of tiny engines

as late summer wasps
dressed in danger tape
necks flashing like landing lights
touched-down on the boughs.

I watched them fold away
their skeleton-leaf wings
and dose themselves for days
with bitter salix bark

the way we do
to numb a sting
or open up the pathways
to the heart.

(the acid in willow bark – salicin – resembles the ingredient in aspirin and has been used for centuries as a pain reliever and to strengthen the heart)

Intangible

Mary Rose McCarthy

MY LITTLE TOE HAS BEEN HURTING for the last ten minutes. I said nothing, as I didn't want to hold the walking group up. I've lagged behind to catch my breath and put on a blister pad.

It's the last day of our holiday in Mayo. I wanted to come here for the light. It's our way of recovering from the waste of sperm that refused to take. Fergal is as empty as I am. We grasp at words as ethereal and unattainable as individual drops that form a cloud.

Early every morning I swim in the sea, so like amniotic fluid holding me in its viscous oily sanctuary. I move through and under the water, surface, and there's no trace of where I've just been. Light and air also bathe me, hold me, and retain no trace of me. I long to swim while pregnant, fluids held in fluid. Folds within folds.

Fergal doesn't swim. It's not competitive enough for him.

After my swim, I grab my paints and paper, return to the strand and work and work to capture the transparency, the turbulence, the sheer energy before me. I can never depict it accurately. Something intrinsic is beyond my reach.

In the evenings Fergal cooks. After dinner, we sit on the terrace, sip wine, and watch the sun play colour-by-numbers on the sea's surface, which some evenings is as flat as glass, others as lumpy as porridge. Yet, whatever the surface it reflects the light, a joyful symbiosis of solar and brine. We rarely talk.

Hill walking Fergal calls it. I've come along on this trek for his sake. He's been so patient all week accompanying me to the beach on my morning swims. He spends hours alone reading at the house while I paint. But no matter what he says, this is no hill. This is a mountain. East-west folded on folds, eroded by the ice melt of a climate change event millennia ago. The ice melt gouged vast, tranquil valleys, while throwing up precipitous heaps of sandstone and quartz. Retreating waters left corries and tarns, secret lakes hidden in the heights.

I'd prefer to savour these small mysteries. But the group aim to reach the summit as swiftly as possible then descend equally quickly.

A shroud of mist has descended, transforming the barren, rocky outcrop. I put my boot back on, immediately feel the comfort of the blister pad. Mist is formed of individual drops, no two the same. The veiled light catches on the drops transforming them to multi-faceted gems. The hairs on my arms, vertical from the damp, trap single pearls of moisture. A muffled bleat comes from a sheep in the valley below.

It is impossible to view sperm droplets with the naked eye. Despite their heads and tails, none of them snag in my body. Yet these random cloud-droplets manage to cling to my arms.

I've no idea where I am other than on a very narrow ridge, and according to the leader, we're almost halfway to the summit. This fascination with reaching the peak eludes me; the pounding thud of boots – tramp, tramp, and tramp – seems pointless. A competition of fitness of who will get there first.

The interlude to fix my blister calms me. I turn my face upwards to the misty cloud, relishing the cool on my sweaty face. My upper lip and eyebrows act as impromptu vessels collecting droplets of moisture before they land on my base layer.

I decide to pull out my jacket, as this mist could turn heavy at any moment. Fergal always says that's the trouble with hill walking: 'Without warning the fickle weather can turn treacherous.' While I'm at it, I also gobble half a banana knowing that the others won't stop for a bite until they attain the peak.

They miss so much of this scenery, the acrid smell of heather strewn with sheep droppings. I hear the harsh call of the raven riding thermals somewhere above me.

My womb is an empty cavern. Each month another walk of shame to buy tampons rather than pampers. The red stains testament to my failure to hang onto one of these tadpole-like microscopic creatures. Seven days of cramps, bloating, mood swings, and Fergal's excruciating care.

Time to move on, I'd better catch up with them. What I really want but won't admit it is to retreat down to one of those tranquil valleys, to flop down and just not move.

I'm completely disorientated when I get to my feet. The world has changed in those few minutes. The ethereal mist morphed into blanket-fog so thick I can barely see my hands. There's no way of knowing where the path is. I don't know which way to turn. I recall just how narrow this crest is.

The mist is no longer comforting, there's menace creeping here. I don't know which way to turn, where to step next.

My foot slips. I stagger, try to straighten, lose my grip on the rucksack, it topples off the ridge. There is no sound of it making landfall. My other leg goes from under me. I follow over the edge in a bizarre acrobatic act as if trying to retrieve my backpack. The flap of my open raincoat snags on a gnarled hawthorn. I come to an abrupt halt. My hand slams against rock. The pain shoots up my shoulder and neck. My face bangs into the coarse grass of the sheep-grazed hill.

Don't panic, I remind myself. Whatever else, don't panic. My feet scrabble against stone. There's not enough purchase to pull me up.

I'm abseiling.

Blood trickles into my eye. My left hand is at an odd angle. I scream. The fog snaffles my voice, traps it within the now sinister, folded beauty.

My hand grasps outwards as if I could catch a hold on the mist. My body jerks again then stills. I'm dangling, suspended in this claustrophobic fog. I breathe, tell myself to breathe, deeper, slower.

My raincoat caught on a bit of a tree is the only thing that's saving me from plummeting. Above and below me there is nothing but dense layers of saturated fog. Perhaps that's a mercy. I can't see how far I've slipped or how many more miles there is yet to fall.

I'm sweating, yet chilled by the damp. I can feel my whole body tremble, bruised and sore. With my good arm, I try to reach upwards, grab the twisted tree. If I could just get a grasp on it, I could lever myself up. But nothing, my hand flails in the air, clutches again at nothing.

My breath is ragged. It's hard to breathe. I can't hang here any longer. My legs ache. I'm empty have nothing left.

'Help. Someone. Help.' No one will hear that. I sound like a cat mewling.

The sweat freezes in my armpits and down my ribcage. My teeth knock off each other. I dangle on. I wonder where is Fergal? I've no hope. The branch creaks. There's no time left. Yet I still strain my arm upwards. I want to catch onto something to lever myself up. I glimpse a patch of sky. It's purple-black. It's waiting to rent apart and spill its load.

The hailstones bounce off my face. They sting my eyelids, closed against their sheer force. Something breaks inside me. My petrified body will draggle like a gruesome decoration off the side of this mountain.

'No,' I roar at the obdurate stillness. 'No. Way. Not Now.'

A pebble skitters across my face.

I look up. A black shape emerges among the hailstones. I raise my good arm in a feeble sort of wave.

A large hand grabs my outstretched arm and pulls me up. Fergal. Someone else holds him around the waist and together they land me on the grass, where I lie like a snagged salmon, gasping, almost sobbing.

No one says anything. I'm grateful they allow me time to catch my breath.

'What happened?' Fergal asks

'Stopped to.' Gasp. 'Then mist came down. And it was beautiful so rested a minute.' Gasp, gasp, gasp.

'Say no more for now. You're safe, no need to fret.'

One of the others arrives, with one of those silver space blankets. Fergal holds a cup of something hot and syrupy sweet against my chattering teeth, and makes me take small sips.

There, there, he says after each one.

Between that and the thermal rug thing, I feel like a small child.

The sky clears and the hail streaks in rods across the reeks. The shaking starts again. I stand up. I try to walk; my legs feel as if they don't belong to me. Something heavy and awkward anchors my ankles.

'Take it easy,' Fergal says. 'We'll get you sorted. Your left wrist is at a very strange angle. It might be broken. Your breathing's not great either.'

Fergal's a volunteer with search and rescue. There's a first-aid kit in his rucksack. He fashions a sling for my left arm. Turns to the others all gathered round and explains there's no need for everyone to turn back. He will get me to safety, the rest should continue on up as planned, make up for lost time.

I hear the note of authority and see the others listen and nod their assent. It's a side of Fergal I've not seen before. The calm, low voice, the gentle way he tucks my arm across my chest and pins the sling at the elbow.

But more than that, I notice the respect he commands among the others. He's not the walk leader, but he's more experienced and takes control of this situation. I've been with Fergal almost three years. We've settled into a comfortable way of acquiescing to each other's needs, without smothering or demanding. It's interesting to see how he marshals others to do his bidding.

Fergal walks on my right, bearing most of my weight. I lean into him as we hobble along. For the first time in ages, we intuitively fit together. But the path is rough and tough going. Each jolt is like electric shocks through my body. I try not to wince or groan but am not always successful. Each time I close my eyes it all replays. It's a mind film of the fall, mist, and that stunted tree. I'd pinned my hopes on something so insubstantial. My muscles won't stop shaking.

At the hospital the triage nurse replaces the sling with something sturdier.

'It's definitely broken,' she says. There's a long wait this evening, though. I'm sorry. It's the usual chaos in here.'

She sighs and directs me to the waiting area, before calling 'next' in a voice heavy with weariness.

Fergal sits beside me, his touch light on my right arm. It's safe and reassuring.

'What did you mean,' he asks, 'when you roared no, not now?'

'You heard that?' I ask.

Then I'm silent. I'm not sure what I meant, other than rebellion at what seemed an inevitable outcome.

'I suppose it just seemed a miserable way to die. What a stupid, silly, mistake to lose my footing, and end up freezing to death, suspended by a coat tail. Careless, that's what it was, careless.'

What I don't say, can't say, is that it felt like yet another way of letting Fergal down.

Again, I hear the baa baaing of the sheep, the crake of the raven, both oblivious to my predicament. My stomach drops, my mouth is dry.

Fergal sighs, and says, 'But I've told you never to separate from the group.'

There it is again, the disappointment in his voice, the strained resignation on his face. Quickly he rearranges his features, laces his fingers in mine. 'Never mind, what's done is done, we'll fare better next time.'

His persistent optimism erodes me.

I don't say, can't say, 'But did you even notice my absence?'

Within Two Kilometres

Sighle Meehan

I can walk by the curve of the sea
to a city sleeping in the summer dust.
Shop fronts bravely showcase
new season must-haves,
pubs entice with ale and Guinness,
restaurants call in Irish, Italian, Chinese,
Aran sweaters pose in hope.
All is entreaty.
Scraps of paper lie lazy in the doorways,
menus yellow in the waiting windows,
empty streets chalk down
another layer of history.

I can walk uphill, through the intersection
to a cemetery rumbling with admonition.
I told you pushing through the clay.
The rainy-day soothsayers
sitting bolt upright now, I'd say,
index bones pointing to the space
where nothing's saved beneath the mattress,
no ditches shored to keep the fox at bay.

Today I walk west.
The air is crisp, clean on my face.
A sparkling sea pokes in and out
through scrubland bright with whins.
Jackdaws swagger on the open road.
A cuckoo calls nearby. May spills out
her trinkets, daisies, buttercups, her wrap
of pink-red clover, cowslip heirlooms.
Three donkeys bunch together, lean their necks
on a stone wall green with lichen,
watch the world breathe easy.

Rendezvous

Giles Newington

They came back, and this time, luckily,
had nothing to say; together walked
in amiable unearthly silence
out of the calm sea.

Father, two mothers, doomed friend, lost lover,
all turned up for the rendezvous; none
cared to win or lose now, nor seek out
secrets to uncover.

Emptied out to a simple silhouette,
hands linked like a child's paper cutout,
blurred by sunlight, they ran to me,
delivered from regret.

The Garden of Earthly Delights

Fiona Pitt-Kethley

I mostly swim quite early in the day.
There's space. The bay is almost empty then.
One night, hoping to see the Perseids we went
just before sundown to enjoy this scene.
As usual I swam out to the barrier
as I came back the light was fading fast,
the beach was packed with partying families,
small groups and clusters, lighting barbecues,
some well-equipped, others with coals on rocks,
fanning the flames, hoping to cook a feast.
Inflatables of every type and shape
beached from the sea, were drawn up here and there,
rings, horses, unicorns and blow-up chairs.
Something about the grouping of this scene
reminded me of Bosch. All life was there.
We lay back on the grit and searched the sky,
shutting out all the busy scene around.
Clouds parted, tiny stars flashed through the sky.

Someday I'll Love Susan Rich

Susan Rich

after Roger Reeves

Often a woman struggles to mention herself.
She hems and haws like a blackbird,
her gaze turned downwards to the glitter of a pie
tin or caught by the brass bell hanging from the door
of her dad's corner store. The bird isn't dumb.
It knows that wanting has its own rock bottom
which no tool or stratagem can fix.
Eventually the hawk shows up
in swan's clothing; eventually the garden
fills with chipped mirrors and cracked
dinner plates. But what's wrong with that?
Why not make a collage of wanting?
Isn't it worse not to want? So what
if it ends in disaster? If we finish
in shelter-in-place with only a blue pier
of desire, a Legend song
and an evening stroll along the shoreline –
won't it still have been worth it?
I have this idea that I might survive;

find myself brighter than a bumblebee's folly.
Even if I remember none of this;
if the clouds mask the Olympic range
and the air transubstantiates to bread soup –
I am still one superhighway
of flesh and fingertips and kaleidoscopic vision.
Someday, my name and I will enlist
all these selves – we'll sign the page
for a lifetime membership to exist
in a seal's call, the tail of a cascade fox.

Visualisation

Lisa C. Taylor

She says, *envision your pain*
outside your body
so, I put it
in the shed west
of my property,
rough-shingled,
slightly askance shelter
that teens discovered
years ago,
then claimed for weekend parties,
their din stretched gauzy
over the maples, to a row
of juniper,

by the old dog house
where my collie used to nap,
her paws extended over the lip
of wood intended
to keep out drizzle
though water seeped
into the structure every spring,
swelling the roof with dark trails
of exposed nails.

The shed, better constructed,
welcomed an old mattress,
cans and bottles,
condom wrappers, hair ties,
and a blue candle in a jelly jar,
matches left
for the next person
to smoke something
or drop at the edge of winter
when dryness became its own season

and yellow-orange fire
snapped and blazed,
like manufactured stars
falling up,
before fizzling,

the pain now skittering
across the frozen ground.

Homing Salmon

Niamh Twomey

Under the gush of shower water your greying skin
flails. In your mind you wade back to the brook,
the water icy even in summer, your seven siblings
balancing on the pebbled belly of the River Fergus,
suds in your hair, brothers dunking you under, ice forming
in your brain, penetrating your veins, Mother shouting *Don't
catch colds*. No one but the river ever taught you how to swim.
Sometimes a silver fish would scurry by upriver. Everyone would freeze,
crane for a glance before it flickered past. *Salmon*, Father said.
Your brothers always poked the verge with sticks, boasted they could catch it.
Their brittle frames have since sailed over the shoulders of their sons
to the graveyard by the river but you remember them young.
Under the gush of shower water your greying scales
glisten in autumn sun.

Growing Pains

Anne Walsh Donnelly

I strode into the fog,
scissors cutting through parchment.
Its low opacity allowed
a forest to form.

I scraped moss that measled
a pine's trunk, tore
at the dark bark; it crumbled
like shortcake biscuits.

I bore a hole through the rings
of many winters, thick resin oozed
out. I watched it make its way
down the trunk like an overweight slug.

My heart emptied and spring sun
entered. I lay on the forest floor,
ear to ground, listened to the trees'
growing pains and remembered mine.

Frances Farmer So You Wanna Be in Pictures

Kevin Kiely

To be alone is to believe no footsteps will approach your door
and grief-school opens with exercises in self-pity
sorrows arrive with the magpies and the rain
the streetlights glare through the wire-glass panels
the plain room is a danger zone
come in and sing Aura Lee *while you hold a glass of wine*
sing it for me, I promise you no conflict, no argument
I want to hear your every word

Frances, so you didn't want to be in those pictures
the movie titles burlesque and mock your life story

Exclusive
Rhythm on the Range
Too Many Parents
The Toast of New York
Ebb Tide
Ride a Crooked Mile
Among the Living
The Party Crashers
No Escape

but you had to lick the academy of motion pictures
in *Makeup* they pluck eyebrows, in *Wardrobe* the carpenters
and paintshop boys peek, flirt and tug your slinky robe

It's a circus Frances, an assembly line, the pretence to sing
through the 1930s; what is an actress but a clothes hanger
arts gratia artis on a napkin for the ashtray

And your Chaplinesque sob-story family plotline:
the harridan mother Lillian, and the scared-off, sly runaway Pa
a recipe for melodrama without a drop of Shakespeare

Loose Rock

Ellen Kelly

I AM A FATHER AND I WAS THERE. I am not the father of either child involved but being the father of any child lends rights. Rights I didn't act upon. That none of the other parents acted upon. But I can only speak for myself. I was there and I knew. I could see. If I'd spoken up I would not be telling this now. It replays over and over. I see it from every angle. Most of all, lately though, I see it from above. As if I'm one of the seagulls hovering, shrieking for it to stop. It was that clear. Perhaps by telling it the shrieking will lessen.

It's a heatwave and we're out here in Connemara with the glorious Twelve Pins cushioning the bay. The cloudless sky renders the ocean turquoise. The sands are white and in some parts a touch golden. You'd never believe that it's Ireland we're in at all. Sure where else in the world would you want to be? This line is bandied about all around us. The other campers along with ourselves. Nobody can believe the luck we're after getting. It is not a campsite we're on. It is a tumbling commonage with donkeys, sheep, cows and a burly rust-coloured bull. No facilities. No shops. Just a handful of campers spread out so that we all have our privacy, our own little bit of heaven.

It's the high tide that draws the strands together. There's an outcrop of rocks. Black with streaks of white, instead of the usual grey. Crevasses sprout little yellow flowers. Somehow little bits of cream and russet Connemara marble find their way here too. I go down with the twins – Fionn and Lorcan – so that they can leap in. It's my job to bring them down and back again safely.

She doesn't like to watch. There are two main jumping spots. Fionn and Lorcan are not allowed to jump from the higher one – a spot with craggy juts of jagged rock over-hanging shallower water.

It just doesn't sit well with her. Other campers and holidaymakers wend their way to the spot like Teletubbies descending the grassy headland. Only they're all in black. The wet-suit brigade. From above the black suits on black rocks might even be indistinguishable. From above it is perhaps only Jamie Horan that stands out.

Fionn and Lorcan have had two jumps already when Jamie shows up. It's as if someone has flicked a switch. Jamie's presence turns up the volume, turns up the light. He's fifteen or maybe sixteen now this year. Lean. Tanned. Black hair with twinkly dark blue eyes. Long coral swim-shorts. A white t-shirt. The younger kids – my two included – look up to him. It's as if as soon as he arrives, the anticipation of real fun comes along too. All around me kids are smiling and laughing. Then without warning, Jamie does a double back-flip off the rocks. I let out a roar. I'm not sure why. Something primal, fear or pride. Like a gorilla in the jungle watching one of the pack take a leap out of a tree, beating his chest. I grab hold of Fionn's arm in case she's watching. I close my eyes. I won't open them until I hear the clap. And it comes, along with whistles. Jamie Horan scrambles back up the black rocks like a mountain goat, beaming from ear to ear. Fionn is one of the whistlers. It's hard not to be one of the whistlers. I whisper into his ear. 'You're never allowed to do that, or anything like it', and I wink at him. A straight jump is all she'll permit.

There's a ripple effect now. There's always a ripple effect in the wake of Jamie Horan. He stands there shivering, his t-shirt stuck to his chest, taut and firm, pubescent nipples pricking through the white wet material. He shakes himself off like a dog before letting a wide yawn and I yawn too, just a little one. Margaret Faherty and I fall into chat while the youngsters queue up for their jumps. She has a bar of Cadbury's Dairy Milk on her.

'For the kids,' she says, laughing, splitting it with me.

'Something about being out here on the rocks has me starving.' She smiles at me. Her teeth are coated in melted brown. I dissolve a square myself, sucking on it to make it last. It lodges on the roof of my mouth, diminishing slowly, dripping its feelgood factors through me.

Jamie is up at the high rock. He stands on his tippy toes and his calf muscles protrude like crescent moons. He takes a run and jumps, spinning around as he goes down in a tornado swirl.

'He puts the heart across me,' I say to Margaret.

'He's great craic, but I know what you mean,' she says.

Lorcan cups his hands over his mouth and shouts out, 'How do you do that, Jamie?' He's starstruck. Jamie is swimming now, big white teeth glinting up at us.

'What, that?' he shouts up. 'That's nothing. Want to see me spin some more?' I do, I'm pretty sure. 'No thanks,' I mutter and Margaret laughs. I scan around for his parents. No sign.

Fionn is pointing and shouting now too. 'Jellyfish, jellyfish, look out, Jamie.' In the clear turquoise water they're easy to spot.

'It's a lion's mane, Jamie, you'd better get out,' Margaret calls down to him.

'A lion's mane? Who's afraid of a little old lion's mane?' Jamie calls up. I am, for one, but nobody says a word. Nobody takes another jump either. This could signal the end of the high-tide activity. My job of getting them back to her safely is done. She'll send me off for the driftwood then so we can get the cooking under way. Rashers, eggs, baked beans. At least they all cook up quickly enough.

Jamie is out of the water, scaling back up the rocks but not smiling his usual smile. He can see we're packing up.

'Hang on, guys,' he says, running now. He lifts a loose rock. He has it up above his head and he's running back down towards the water. Then he hurls the rock in shouting 'take that, lion's mane,' and he pencil dives into the ocean, cutting it clean. As if he's an Olympian.

'Christ, what next?' I say to Margaret, rubbing my arms, watching the spot he entered.

'That jellyfish is going off like the clappers,' she says, laughing.

Jamie Horan bursts back out of the water with the rock in his hands. Every single person out here claps him. I look down at my own hands. They're stinging from the hard slap I've just given them. A few of the kids begin to chant.

Go Jamie, go Jamie, go Jamie.

Some of the adults too. Some of the adults are definitely chanting too. I'm not sure if I'm one of them. Jamie does it again. Hurl. Dive. Retrieve. Beam.

'I think we can safely say you scared the daylights out of it, Jamie,'

Margaret calls down to him. The clapping again. The chanting again. He's getting tired now, flagging a little bit, I can tell. But he will not disappoint. Instead of hurling it this time he rolls it off the rocks. He jumps in after it, brings it back up bursting out of the water to some fading claps. The jellyfish has gone. There's no need for him to continue with this. Somebody needs to tell him.

'He could give that a rest now Margaret, with the kids starting to jump again,' I say. She can tell him. She seems to have an ease with him. It would sound better coming from her. A bit gruff from me, I tell myself. Instead she does what I did earlier. Scans around for his parents. Neither of us thinks we can tell him to stop. Margaret's John takes a leap, hot-tailed by Fionn and then Lorcan. Jamie is positioning himself for another roll of the rock. I'm feeling dizzy watching him now. Watching them. Watching him. Dizzy and knotted with nerves or something. I'm looking left to the kids and right to him. A sentry on guard. A nauseous, wuss of a sentry. He rolls. He jumps.

At first it is as if a rain cloud has sprung above the rocks, muddying the clear water. But John Faherty is shouting, bellowing, and swimming frantically towards the spot where Jamie is supposed to be surfacing. The cloud is in the water, a deep purple, spreading quickly through the turquoise. Margaret Faherty is running and a low guttural noise – like a donkey braying – is coming from her. I am frozen to the spot. I think that it is Jamie. But then he bursts through the bloodied water.

'I can't see it,' he shouts up to us. Up to the silence. Except for the braying. He's swinging his head around and then he sees. Just as we all see. John Faherty breaking through the water's surface with his sister in his arms. The blood streams through her long honey hair. John passes little Ann up to Margaret. Up to the high-pitched wail which is now coming from her as she kneels down and cradles her daughter. I fumble with my phone, pressing 999 again and again but there's no signal out here on the rocks. So I scramble up and over and I run across the headland until I see the little bars appearing and I ring, calling down the line that a seven-year-old girl has a severe trauma to the head out on the rocks in the bay. That an ambulance will never find us on time. That they'll have to send the helicopter. I run back down to Margaret, my arms flailing uselessly and I swing them around her and cup my hands to catch some of the blood, as if that will help. She's rocking back and forth, mumbling those words.

Little Ann Faherty hadn't learnt to swim strongly yet. She wasn't going to be doing any jumping at full tide. But on that day, three years ago to the day, she was going to try something different. Instead of splashing around within her depth in the cove with her friends she had made her way across to the lower rocks, hidden by the higher juts. When John leapt in he saw her there, hovering. Then she smiled at him, put her arms in a triangle and swam one stroke out towards him.

The Coroner's Court recorded a verdict of accidental death. This is not an accurate verdict. Death by adult passivity. That's what I call it. His parents, who must've known. They've a hand in it. But they weren't there. I've the biggest hand in it. Bigger than Jamie himself. I was there and I am an adult and I did not try to stop him. Shrouded in a veil of political correctness. That's how I see it when I'm being kind to myself in the daylight hours. When I can push what else I know back down. Because the truth is worse than that. Even in the re-telling I can feel it. Even as Margaret Faherty's words spin in me, first thing, last thing, right through the night. Rasping and hissing. The full effect of his beauty on me plain to us both.

Artist's Statement
Béatrice Mecking

Originally from Fair-Isle in the Acadian Peninsula of New Brunswick, Canada, **Béatrice Mecking** now lives in Tabusintac, NB. She studied art at the New Brunswick Community College and took courses in Dramatic Arts at the University of Moncton (1979). She then gave puppet shows in schools, which she performed, wrote and made the puppets and sets. Béatrice's art is reflected by the symbols, materials and textures present in her works. With a strong thirst for discovery, she is inspired by the emotions of humour, irony and injustice that strongly affect her.

Her work is also influenced by her Acadian roots. Acadians are descended from the French settlers to eastern Canada in the early 18th century. They have been known for their survival in harsh environments, generosity and sense of fun. Beatrice's grandfather Jeffrey Breau was a farmer and a blacksmith. Many Acadians were fishermen. The expulsion of the Acadians by the British took place in 1755. Thousands were sent back to France or to other French territories such as Louisiana (Acadians-Cajuns). Beatrice's family hid in the woods and were helped by the local native peoples, the Mi'kmaq.

Biographical Details

Deborah Bacharach is the author of *After I Stop Lying* (Cherry Grove Collections, 2015). She received a 2020 Pushcart honourable mention and has been published in journals such as *The Adroit Journal*, *Poetry Ireland Review*, *Vallum*, *The Carolina Quarterly*, and *The Southampton Review* among many others. She is an editor, teacher and tutor in Seattle. DeborahBacharach.com.

Peter Branson is a former teacher and lecturer in English Literature and tutor in creative writing and poetry. He is now a full time poet, songwriter and traditional-style singer. His poetry has been published in Britain, USA, Canada, Ireland, Australia, New Zealand and South Africa, including in *Acumen*, *Agenda*, *Ambit*, *Envoi*, *The London Magazine*, *Reach*, *Sarasvati*, *The Warwick Review*, *Iota*, *Frogmore Papers*, *The Interpreter's House*, *Magma*, *Poetry Nottingham*, *South*, *Elbow Room*, *The Curlew*, *The Fenland Reed*, *The New Writer*, *Crannóg*, *Measure*, *The Raintown Review*, *The Houston Poetry Review*, *Barnwood*, *Main Street Rag*, *The Able Muse* and *Other Poetry*. His *Red Hill, Selected Poems* was published in 2013 by Lapwing, Belfast. His latest collection, *Hawk Rising*, also from Lapwing, was published in 2016. He has won prizes and been placed in a number of competitions over recent years, including a 'highly commended' in the Petra Kenny International, first prizes in the Grace Dieu and the Envoi International and a special commendation in the 2012 Wigtown. He was shortlisted for the 2018/19 Poetry Business Pamphlet and Collection competition.

Dylan Brennan was awarded the Ireland Chair of Poetry Bursary Award in 2019 by Ireland Chair of Poetry Eiléan Ní Chuilleanáin. His debut poetry collection, *Blood Oranges*, was published by The Dreadful Press in 2014 and was awarded the Patrick Kavanagh Award runner-up prize. In 2017 he collaborated on *Guadalupe & Other Hallucinations*, a series of exhibitions and an illustrated e-book, with Belfast-based visual artist Jonathan Brennan. In 2016 he co-edited *Rethinking Juan Rulfo's Creative World: Prose, Photography, Film* with Prof. Nuala Finnegan (UCC), a volume of academic essays on the work of Mexican writer/photographer Juan Rulfo. He has been invited to read at major literary festivals in Columbia, Nicaragua, Mexico, Italy, Ireland and the USA (O'Miami) and has twice been a recipient of a Culture Ireland Travel Grant.

Michael Brown's work has been published widely in magazines including *The Rialto*, *Southword*, *The North* and others. He was selected by Clare Pollard for a Northern Writers' Award (New North Poets) in 2017. He was placed second in York Poetry competition 2019. He has twice been shortlisted in the Basil Bunting Award and in 2018 won the Wirral Firsts Poetry Competition and was commended in the McLellan Prize by Sinead Morrissey. His pamphlets *Undersong* (2014) and *Locations for a Soul* (2016) are available from Eyewear Publishing and Templar respectively. His first collection, *Where Grown Men Go*, was published by Salt in Autumn 2019.

Edel Burke lives in Castlebar, Co. Mayo. She is winner of Dromineer Poetry Competition 2017, was highly commended iYeats Poetry 2017 and Over the Edge, short story, 2014. She has been published in *Something About Home, New Writing on Migration and Belonging, Crannóg 45, The Rush Anthology, Boyne Berries – The Ledwidge Issue* and *Banshee*.

David Butler's novel *City of Dis* was shortlisted for the Irish Novel of the Year, 2015. His stories have won the Edgeworth, Fish and Redline short story awards.

Lynn Caldwell's work is forthcoming in *Crosswinds Poetry Journal* and has been published in Dedalus Press's anthology *WRITING HOME*; *The Irish Times* for March 2019's Hennessy New Irish Writing Award, *Cassandra Voices*, and *The Antigonish Review*, and has featured on RTÉ's *Sunday Miscellany*. She was a runner up in Aesthetica's Creative Writing Award 2017. She blogs at https//kennedystreet. wordpress. com.

Bernie Crawford lives in Co. Galway and in 2019 was awarded a bursary by Galway County Council. Her poetry has been published extensively including in *New Irish Writing* in the *Irish Times, Poetry Ireland Review, the North* magazine, *Mslexia, Stony Thursday Book*, and *Crannóg*. She won first place in Poetry Ireland/Trócaire competition in 2017. A selection of her poetry is featured in *The Blue Nib Chapbook 3*. She is on the editorial board of the poetry magazine *Skylight 47*.

Emily Cullen is a Galway-based writer, curator, harper and scholar. She has published three poetry collections, *Conditional Perfect* (Doire Press, 2019), *In Between Angels and Animals* (Arlen House, 2013) and *No Vague Utopia* (Ainnir Publishing, 2003). *Conditional Perfect* was included in *The Irish Times'* roundup of 'the best new poetry of 2019'. She was Director of Cúirt International Festival of Literature between 2017 and 2019 and she currently teaches creative writing at NUI Galway.

Stephen de Búrca is currently working on his first poetry collection after earning his MFA in poetry at the University of Florida. He won the poetry award for the 2019 *Over The Edge New Writer of the Year*. His poetry has also appeared or is forthcoming in *Fish Anthology 2019, Crannóg, The Honest Ulsterman, Boyne Berries, Abridged*, and *Skylight 47*.

Honor Duff has had poetry published in *Crannóg, The Stony Thursday Book, Skylight 47* and *Boyne Berries*. She is a member of The Cavan-Meath LitLab Writers Group.

Rory Duffy has had work published in several journals including *Southword, Crannóg, The Stony Thursday Book, A New Ulster, Skylight 47, Boyne Berries* and *The Cormorant*. He has been shortlisted in Cúirt, Sean O'Faoláin, PJ O'Connor, Frances MacManus, Over The Edge, Bath Short Story Award, among others. In 2017 he was nominated for a ZeBBie Award by the Irish Writers Guild for *Paulo in the Underworld* (a radio play). In 2018 he was commended in the Gregory O'Donohue

Prize. In 2019 he won the Red Line Book Festival Poetry Prize and was second in the Strokestown Summer Poetry Award.

Frank Dullaghan is an Irish Writer currently locked down in Kuala Lumpur, Malaysia. Cinnamon Press has published four of his collections, most recently *Lifting the Latch* (2018). His work is widely published in journals, including in *Cyphers*, *HU*, *London Magazine*, *Magma*, *New Welsh Review*, *Nimrod*, *Poetry Bus*, *Poetry Review*, and *Rattle*.

Billy Fenton lives outside Waterford City and he writes poetry and short stories. His work has been published in the *Irish Times*, *Poetry Ireland Review*, *Crannóg*, *Honest Ulsterman*, *Bangor Literary Journal* and others. He was shortlisted for a Hennessy Award in 2018.

Cian Ferriter won the Westival 2019 International Poetry Competition, was a runner-up in the Gregory O'Donoghue International Poetry Competition 2020 and has had poems accepted for publication in Irish and international poetry journals.

Vincent Glynn-Steed's work has appeared in journals and online sites in the United States, Mexico, Wales, England and Northern Ireland. Publications include: *Crannóg*, *Into the Void*, *Boyne Berries*, *Skylight 47*, *Parhelion*, *Mediterranean Poetry*, *Ofi Press Magazine*, *Galway Review*, *Headstuff*, *Cinnamon Press*, *Ogham Stone* to name but a few. Maytree Press will publish his debut chapbook *Catching Air* later this year.

Caroline Graham's short fiction has been published in *Crannóg*, *Revival*, *Boyne Berries* and various anthologies. She has also published non-fiction and academic articles and has co-edited two books. She is a co-founder of the Regional Writing Centre at the University of Limerick and was Chair of the Literature and Writing Committee for Limerick City of Culture 2014. She is currently a member of a peer critique group at the Limerick Writers' Centre and a professional member of the Irish Writers' Centre, including the WORD forum.

David C. Hall has published novels and short stories in both Spanish and English. In 2017 he won the José Maria Valverde Prize for a short collection of poems in Spanish. In English he has published poetry in *Driftwood Press*, *Columbia Poetry Review*, *The New Guard*, and *Into the Void*.

Hanahazukashi is a theatre maker, teacher, and member of Galway Writers' Workshop. She is chairperson of Theatre Room Galway where she writes, directs, and acts. She has written for HeadStuff.org and been published in *Crannóg*. She was long-listed for Over the Edge Writer of the Year, and placed second for reading her piece, *Presyncope*, during Culture Night in 2017. She is currently editing her first novel.

Gerard Hanberry is a prizewinning poet published by Salmon Poetry currently working on his fifth poetry collection. He also writes non-fiction. His most recent publication is *On Raglan Road – Great Irish Love Songs and the Women Who Inspired Them* (The Collins Press / Gills).

John Higgins is a 23-year-old Irish writer. His work has been featured in *Honest Ulsterman, New Pop Lit, The Blue Nib* and more. He lives in Galway.

Kevin Higgins is co-organiser of Over The Edge literary events in Galway. He has published five full collections of poems: *The Boy With No Face* (2005), *Time Gentlemen, Please* (2008), *Frightening New Furniture* (2010), *The Ghost in the Lobby* (2014), Sex *and Death at Merlin Park Hospital* (2019). His poems also feature in *Identity Parade – New British and Irish Poets* (Bloodaxe, 2010) and in *The Hundred Years' War: Modern War Poems* (Ed Neil Astley, Bloodaxe May 2014). Kevin was satirist-in-residence with the alternative literature website The Bogman's Cannon 2015–16. *The Selected Satires of Kevin Higgins* was published by NuaScéalta in 2016. *Song of Songs 2:0 – New & Selected Poems* was published by Salmon in Spring 2017. Kevin is a highly experienced workshop facilitator and several of his students have gone on to achieve publication success. He has facilitated poetry workshops at Galway Arts Centre and taught Creative Writing at Galway Technical Institute for the past fifteen years. He is the Creative Writing Director for the NUI Galway International Summer School and also teaches on the NUIG BA Creative Writing Connect programme. His poems have been praised by, among others, Tony Blair's biographer John Rentoul, *Observer* columnist Nick Cohen, writer and activist Eamonn McCann, historian Ruth Dudley Edwards, and *Sunday Independent* columnist Gene Kerrigan; and have been quoted in *The Daily Telegraph*, *The Independent*, *The Times* (London), *Hot Press* magazine, *The Daily Mirror* and on *The Vincent Browne Show*. *The Stinging Fly* magazine has described Kevin as 'likely the most widely read living poet in Ireland'. His most recent poetry collection *Sex and Death at Merlin Park Hospital* was published by Salmon Poetry in June; one of the poems from which will feature in *A Galway Epiphany*, the final instalment of Ken Bruen's Jack Taylor series of novels. His work has been broadcast on RTÉ Radio, Lyric FM, and BBC Radio 4.

Maria Isakova Bennett is an artist and writer from Liverpool, works for charities and creates a hand-stitched poetry journal, *Coast to Coast to Coast*. She received a Northern Writers' Award in 2017/18, and was invited to be poet and artist-in-residence at Poetry-in-Aldeburgh for 2018. For the festival she created a litany of work by 48 poets from the UK, Ireland, and France. During 2019, she worked with poet John Glenday to create his latest pamphlet *mira* and an exhibition of accompanying art pieces. Her pamphlets are: *Caveat* (2015); *All of the Spaces* (2018); *… an ache in each welcoming kiss (2019)*.

Fred Johnston was the founder of Galway's Cúirt Festival. His most recent collection of poems is *Rogue States* (Salmon Poetry 2019).

Miceál Kearney has published two collections of poetry. *Inheritance* (Doire Press, 2008) and *The Inexperienced Midwife* (Arlen House, 2016). He is currently working on his third collection: *Set in Stone*. He has also had four short plays staged.

John D. Kelly's work won the Listowel Short Collection Prize, 2020 and the Desmond O'Grady competition, 2020, and is included in many literary publications and anthologies. His first collection *The Loss of Yellowhammers* was recently published (2020) by Summer Palace Press.

Ellen Kelly is a sociologist, writer and blogger. Her competition-winning short stories have been published online, in an anthology, in *The Irish Times* and in *Crannóg*. She was shortlisted for the inaugural Sunday Business Post/Penguin Ireland award in 2016 and the Hennessy New Irish Writing award in 2018. She has had a story broadcast on RTÉ Radio 1 as part of the Francis MacManus competition. She is completing her first novel.

Kevin Kiely holds a PhD from University College Dublin, an MPhil from Trinity College (Dublin). He is a W.J. Fulbright Scholar in Poetry, Washington (DC), and an Hon. Fellow in Writing, University of Iowa. He is a commentator on poetry, literature and the arts in *Village: Politics and Culture* among other publications. His books include: *UCD Belfield Metaphysical: A Retrospective* (Lapwing Press), *Harvard's Patron: Jack of All Poets* (Areogapitica Publishing), *SOS Lusitania* (O'Brien Press), *Breakfast with Sylvia* (Lagan Press, Belfast). He was awarded five Arts Council Literature Bursary Awards, a Patrick Kavanagh Fellowship in Poetry, and a Bisto Award for *A Horse Called El Dorado* (O'Brien Press). www.kevinkiely.net

Patrick Kehoe's debut collection, *It's Words You Want*, was published in 2011 by Salmon Poetry. His second book of poetry, *The Cask of Moonlight*, was published by Dedalus Press in 2014. He wrote the lyrics for Sonny Condell's songs as featured on the album *Seize the Day* (2017). His most recent collection, *Places to Sleep*, was published by Salmon Poetry in 2018.

Adina Kopinsky is an emerging poet living in Israel. She has work published or forthcoming in *Glass: A Journal of Poetry*, *Rust + Moth*, and *SWWIM Every Day*, among other publications.

Mercedes Lawry is the author of *Small Measures*, forthcoming from Twelve Winters Press, and three chapbooks, the latest, *In the Early Garden with Reason*, which was selected by Molly Peacock for the 2018 WaterSedge Chapbook Contest. Her poetry has appeared in such journals as *Poetry*, *Nimrod*, and *Prairie Schooner*. Her work has been nominated five times for a Pushcart Prize and her fiction was a semi-finalist in The Best Small Fictions 2016. Additionally, she has published stories and poems for children.

Mary Rose McCarthy has been awarded The Golden Pen, The Kenny/Naughton prize, and the Amergin prize. She has twice been longlisted for the RTÉ Guide/Penguin short story prize. Her work has been published in *Crannóg* and *Boyne Berries*.

Sighle Meehan's poems have been published in magazines and anthologies including *Poetry Ireland Review*, *The Stinging Fly*, *Skylight 47*, *Crannóg*, *Fish Anthology*, *Best British and Irish Poets 2019* (Eyewear), and *Universal Oneness*

(New Delhi). She was winner or runner up/shortlisted in competitions including iYeats, Over The Edge New Writer, McLellan, Fish and Shirley McClure.

Mary Melvin Geoghegan has five collections of poetry published, her most recent, *As Moon and Mother Collide*, with Salmon Poetry (2018). Her work has been widely published including in *Poetry Ireland Review*.

Rachel Morton graduated with a degree in English from the University of Melbourne in 2004 and completed a master's degree in Applied Linguistics in 2009. In 2019 she was shortlisted for the Australian Catholic University Prize for Poetry.

Giles Newington worked for nearly twenty years as a journalist at *The Irish Times* and has had work published in *Abridged*, *Crannóg*, *Dublin Review of Books* and *The Honest Ulsterman*.

Úna Ní Cheallaigh holds an MA in Creative Writing from UCC. Her poetry has been published in *The Irish Times*, *The Stony Thursday Book*, *The Quarry Man*, *The North*, *Orbis*, *Poetry Salzburg* and *Washing Windows*, (Arlen House). She was shortlisted for Poems for Patience 2019.

Fiona Nic Dhonnacha holds an MA in Literature and Publishing and writes both poetry and short stories.

Rachel Parry was shortlisted and published in the Poets Meet Politics International Poetry Competition Anthology in 2018. She was placed first in the Fish Lockdown Poetry Prize. She is also a visual artist.

Fiona Pitt-Kethley is the author of more than twenty books of poetry or prose.

Kate Quigley is a graduate of NUI Galway's BA Connect with Creative Writing. Her work has been published in a number of Irish and UK journals including *The Stinging Fly*, *Orbis*, *Banshee* and *THE SHOp*. Her debut poetry pamphlet, *If You Love Something*, was published by Rack Press in October 2019.

Ruth Quinlan was selected for the Heinrich Böll Cottage Writer Residency in 2020, the Poetry Ireland Introductions Series in 2019 and was awarded an individual artist bursary in 2018 by Galway City Council. She won the 2018 Galway University Hospital Arts Trust Poems for Patience competition, the 2018 Blue Nib Summer Chapbook competition, the 2014 Over the Edge New Writer of the Year Award, and the 2012 Hennessy Literary Award for First Fiction. She is also co-editor of *Skylight 47*, a poetry magazine based in Galway.

Susan Rich is the author of four books of poetry, most recently *Cloud Pharmacy* (shortlisted for the Julie Suk Prize) and *The Alchemist's Kitchen* (finalist for the Washington State Book Award). She has been granted a Fulbright Fellowship, the PEN USA Award for Poetry, the Times Literary Supplement Award and a 4Culture Grant. Her poems appear in *Crannóg*, *Harvard Review*, *New England Review*, *Poetry Ireland Review*, and *World Literature Today* among many other places. Her collections *A Gallery of Postcards and Maps: New and Selected Poems* (Salmon Press) and *Blue Atlas* (Red Hen Press) are forthcoming.

Knute Skinner, born in America, has had a home in Ireland since 1963. His collected poems, *Fifty Years: Poems 1957–2007*, was published by Salmon Poetry in 2007, *Concerned Attentions* was published by Salmon in 2013, *Against All Odds* was published by Lapwing Publications in 2016, *The Life That I Have* was published by Salmon in 2018, and *An Upside Down World* was published by Salmon in 2019.

Fiona B. Smith has had poetry published in *Poetry Ireland Review*, *Crannóg*, *Southword*, *the Stony Thursday Book*, *Hennessy New Irish Writing*, *The Galway Review* and the Templar Poetry anthology *Skein*. She won the Over the Edge New Writer of the Year poetry section in 2012 and was runner-up in the Goldsmith Poetry Competition 2017. She was selected to read as an emerging poet at the Cork Spring Poetry Festival. She has also read at Kinsale Arts Weekend, Skibbereen Arts Festival, Derwent Poetry Festival, Over the Edge Literary Gathering in Galway.

Gerard Smyth's tenth collection, *The Sundays of Eternity*, was published by Dedalus Press in 2020. His other books include *A Song of Elsewhere* (Dedalus) and *The Yellow River* (with artwork by Seán McSweeney) which was published by Solstice Arts Centre in Navan. He is a member of Aosdána.

Anne Tannam has published two poetry collections: *Take This Life* (Wordsonthestreet, 2011) and *Tides Shifting Across My Sitting Room Floor* (Salmon Poetry, 2017), with a third, *Twenty-six Letters of a New Alphabet*, forthcoming with Salmon Poetry in 2020. www.annetannampoetry.ie

Lisa C. Taylor is the author of four collections of poetry, most recently *Necessary Silence* (Arlen House, 2013) and two short story collections, most recently *Impossibly Small Spaces* (Arlen House, 2018). Her honours include Pushcart nominations in fiction and poetry, a Hugo House New Works Fiction Award, and along with Geraldine Mills, the Elizabeth Shanley Gerson Lecture in Irish Literature at University of Connecticut. Her books have been taught at Norwalk Community College, Manchester Community College, and University of Connecticut. She is an editor for Wordpeace.co and a book reviewer for *Mom Egg Review*. www.lisactaylor.com

Laura Treacy Bentley is a poet, novelist, and amateur photographer from Huntington, West Virginia. She is the author of a poetry art book, *Looking for Ireland: An Irish Appalachian Pilgrimage*, a literary thriller set in Ireland, *The Silver Tattoo*, a short story prequel, *Night Terrors*, and a poetry collection, *Lake Effect*. She was awarded a Fellowship Award for Literature from the West Virginia Commission on the Arts and recently recorded her poem *Seoul* for the West Virginia Humanities Council's online series 'Poetry During a Time of Crisis'. She has been published in the United States and Ireland, and her work has been featured on *A Prairie Home Companion*, *Poetry Ireland Review*, *Poetry Daily*, *Crannóg*, *The Stinging Fly*, and *O Magazine*. lauratreacybentley.com

Iain Twiddy studied literature at university and lived for several years in northern Japan. His poetry has appeared in *Poetry Ireland Review*, *The Stinging Fly*, *The Moth*, and elsewhere.

Niamh Twomey has recently completed an MA in Creative Writing at UCC. Her work has previously featured in journals and anthologies such as *Boyne Berries*, *Poethead*, and many more. She is a regular attender and reader at Cork's Ó Bhéal open mic nights.

Anne Walsh Donnelly writes poetry, prose and plays. She was nominated for the Hennessy/Irish Times Literary Award and selected for the Poetry Ireland Introduction Series in 2019. She is the author of the poetry chapbook *The Woman With an Owl Tattoo* and the short story collection *Demise of the Undertaker's Wife*. annewalshdonnelly.com

Alison Wells lives in Bray. She worked as a technical writer and is now a librarian. She has a postgraduate degree in Psychology and her Head-above-Water blog explores creativity and resilience. Her stories have been shortlisted for, among others, Hennessy New Irish Writing, Bridport, BBC Opening Lines and Bray Literary Festival. Her writing has appeared in *The Stinging Fly*, *The Lonely Crowd*, *Crannóg*, UK National Flash Fiction days anthologies and New Island/RTÉ Arena's *New Planet Cabaret*. In January 2019 her novel *Eat!* was highly commended in the Irish Writers Centre Novel Fair. This year she was selected as a finalist with *The Exhibit of Held Breaths*.

Máiríde Woods writes poetry and short stories. Her work has appeared in anthologies and reviews and has been broadcast on RTÉ radio. She has won several prizes, including two Hennessys, the Francis MacManus and PJ O'Connor awards from RTÉ. Three poetry collections, *The Lost Roundness of the World*, *Unobserved Moments of Change* and *A Constant Elsewhere of the Mind*, have been published by Astrolabe, the last in 2017. In 2019 she had poems published in *Crannóg* and *Poetry Ireland Review*.

Stay in touch with
Crannóg
@
www.crannogmagazine.com

www.ingramcontent.com/pod-product-compliance
Lightning Source LLC
Chambersburg PA
CBHW080940040426
42444CB00015B/3384